Bob & Barbara,

I pray that this book will
be a big blessing to you.

Mark 1:17-18

All the best,

Joe Haavik

To the ends of

the earth

Dedication

To my beautiful, beloved wife, Stephanie.

This story would have been neither experienced nor shared had it not been for our beautiful love story. By God´s loving guidance, He orchestrated the most amazing divine appointment of my entire life when I ran into you in a wedding in Jamaica all those years ago.

Our love story has been a beautiful masterpiece crafted by our Creator from the very start, and I could not be more grateful for the privilege of spending the rest of my life together with you, my helpmate made perfectly fit for me.

You inspire me to be the best I can be, to live life to the fullest and to make a difference in the lives of others.
I love you with all my heart!

To my precious children, Joshua, Adrian and Mia.

You are all so amazing and uniquely created by God our Father to be a light to this world. My love for you goes deeper than life itself, and it is my heart´s desire to see you walk in God´s true purpose for your lives. I am so very proud of each one of you, and I am blessed to be your dad.

Endorsements

"What I love about this book is the absence of religious practices, outlines and rules. This is a story about passion, purpose, fearlessness and faith. The powerful reality is that this story is available to anyone at anytime."

—Pastor IV Marsh, Epic Church, CEO and founder of IAM4 and LeadNow

There are those who talk about missions. There are those who go on mission trips. Both are good and needed. But when you have the rare opportunity to cross paths with someone who actually lives missions, you are in the presence of Faith. Tore is one of those people. The book you are about to read is his story but it is much more than that. It is an authentic, challenging, exciting, unpredictable journey of faith. This story is not just a "good read". It is a living, ongoing adventure that will capture your heart and point you straight to the One who started it all. You will be inspired by reading To the Ends of the Earth.

More importantly, you may discover how God is going to make a difference with your life! "

— Dr. Larry Little, CEO and Founder of Eagle Center for Leadership

"The stories in this book remind me of the book of Acts! When I began reading To The Ends Of The Earth I was immediately captivated by so many examples of radical obedience, miracles, and faith in God. I deeply admire Tore's passionate desire to fearlessly share the Gospel. He is committed to reach the world! To The Ends Of The Earth will inspire you to believe that you can hear God's voice clearly and specifically. You can expect God to show you His destiny for your life!"

— Pastor Steven Charles, Bethesda Church Lindale, TX

"To the Ends of the Earth" is a very inspiring story showing what happened when one man followed the Holy Spirit completely. It is very encouraging to note that we can all experience abundant blessings if we follow God in faith as Tore did.

— Mayor Tab Bowling, City of Decatur, Alabama

"It has been a long time since I could not put a book down. Tore´s story is compelling, fun, and instructive. It draws you in, making you eager to see what will happen next. Tore´s adventurous story demonstrates that all of us can go on a meaningful and effective journey with God – if we will just seek God and walk by faith.

— Pastor Dan Durbin, Executive Pastor Epic Church and Business Consultant LeadNow

Foreword

by Pastor IV Marsh, Lead Pastor of Epic Church

I remember the day Tore gave me this book to read and asked me to write a foreword. To be completely honest, I had this mental struggle I usually have when someone asks me to read a book they have written. I assumed it was going to contain the same boring, vague and typical Christian journey that I have seen time after time.

But when I began to read, I sensed that this book was something very different. I was actually reading about someone who understood the Gospel and what it means to follow the voice of Holy Spirit at all cost. It was inspiring!

As I continued to read I could see how Tore did not write about something he had heard, a theology concept, doctrine or theory. Tore wrote from an endless well of experiences where he had sought God's heart concerning the Gospel. When Holy Spirit spoke, Tore followed. Because of his faith and courage Tore was able to experience and witness God's power, the same power which leads us where He needs us to be in order to reach people that have yet to be reached.

Tore inspires us with a story of how God doesn't require us

to pass some Christian exam in order to be a part of what He is doing. He tells a story where God is looking for someone, anyone, to just be available. God is looking for someone to actually believe Him, not just believe in Him. God is looking for someone to go, no matter the cost.

What I love about this book is the absence of religious practices, outlines and rules. This is a story about passion, purpose, fearlessness and faith. The powerful reality is that this story is available to anyone at anytime. We often want God to show us, or even provide for us before we take that first step of faith. Well, that wouldn't be faith now would it? Just as God told Abraham, "Go from your country, your people and your father's household to a land I will show you," God spoke to Tore to leave all that was comfortable while inviting him on a journey of provision and countless miracles.

So, dive head first into this book and get ready to be inspired to live life to the fullest. Invite others to do the same. What you will see is that what Jesus spoke, "I have come that they may have life and live it to the full," still rings true today to those who dare to follow Him no matter the cost.

-Pastor TV Marsh

"Are you still willing

to go to the

ends of the earth

for Me?"

Chapter One

SPRING WAS FINALLY starting to make its way to the depths of the long Norwegian fjord with its majestic mountains shooting up from the deep trenches of ocean water. Sauda, a small industrial town with only four thousand inhabitants, was still shivering from the cold, dark winter as the beams of sunlight reached our kitchen window. The peaks of the snow-covered mountains surrounding the small town glowed as the sun slowly made its way higher in the blue morning sky. The patches of beautiful, white snowbell flowers decorating our yard were a clear sign that the winter was finally over. It had been the longest and most pain-filled winter of my twenty-one years of life.

A severe back injury had kept me from working my factory job for more than two months now. The pain from lifting much of anything shot like lightning bolts throughout my body, and going back to work at the security glass lamination line was not happening anytime soon. I had been going to both doctors and physical therapists for weeks, but had seen only barely noticeable improvement. I kept finding myself wondering what day of the week it was—they all seemed to run together as my life felt more and more like a maze of discouragement and disappointment. I did find great comfort in talking to my beautiful fiancée, Stephanie, over the phone. She lived about seven hours away, and we were counting down the months until our September wedding, which would take place in Texas later in the year. Today, however, the pain and frustration of my condition had brought me to my knees in prayer and hope for a divine intervention as my eyes welled up with tears.

It was only a little over a year ago that I had traveled throughout Asia with a multinational evangelism team, ministering to thousands of people and seeing God's powerful miracles on every hand. The vivid memories of witnessing to people who had never heard of Christ and seeing them come to faith and experience miraculous healing right in front of my eyes still challenged my faith. The privilege of seeing blind people regain their sight, watching lame people rise to walk and seeing cancer healed in the name of Jesus had radically changed my life and heart for the mission field forever.

I was temporarily living at my parents' house for a few months while putting aside money for my upcoming wedding. Although the stay had allowed me the opportunity to serve as a youth leader at the church my parents pastored, I kept waking up with a feeling that I had left a large piece of my heart behind in Asia. The anticlimax of partaking in powerful miracles and now being the victim of the paralyzing chains of pain was slowly but surely weighing me down since medicine and therapy weren't resulting in recovery.

I had met Stephanie, my fiancée, three years earlier while working as a missionary in Jamaica. She was soon headed to Thailand on a mission trip, and I couldn't have been more thrilled for her. The two-month mission trip was the final step in her discipleship training school, which she had been part of in Skien, Norway, for the last year. Our plan was to have her graduate from school while I worked to save up money for our wedding. It all seemed like a great plan until the day I woke up and found myself unable to get out of bed due to intense back pain. At first I thought it was just a pulled muscle that would heal after a few days of rest. However I quickly realized that whatever was wrong was much more severe than I had first thought.

I was now on my knees, fully dependent on God's intervention, crying out for His healing power to flow through my body and get me back on my feet. In the midst of that dark and painful hour, I felt an immense peace fill the room, and God spoke to me in the depths of my heart. I felt as if He had reached down to dry the tears from my cheeks and wrapped His arms around me as He spoke into my ear.

Since becoming a Christian at the age of fourteen, I had often heard the still, small voice of God during my prayer times, but it sounded as clear this time as it had four years earlier when I was alone on my knees seeking God for direction; then, I had just completed my discipleship training school after a two month mission trip to Ethiopia, and I was debating what to do with my life and whether or not I should go back to school when God clearly told me, "Move to Jamaica and work with children and youth." So although I had learned to recognize His still, small voice and had followed Him with obedience in the past, doubt quickly entered my mind as I heard Him say this time, "Drop everything, and buy a ticket to Hong Kong. I will tell you where to go from there."

I immediately wondered if God was really speaking to me or if I just missed China so much that I wanted Him to tell me to drop my plans and go back there. I asked myself whether this was simply a cry out of the void in my heart created when I left Asia. How could I, in my current condition of pain and despair, even consider heading off to travel the world once again? I wasn't able to lift even a dumbbell off the ground without experiencing extreme agony. How would I be able to carry a backpack? I was also conflicted by the thought of using the hard-earned money I had saved for the wedding. Should I really resign my job only a few months before Stephanie and I were to be married? "God," I prayed, "is this really from You?"

As much as I wanted God to send confirmations my way to prove that He had actually spoken to me, He remained quiet from that moment on—I received no other answer, and no confirmation from His Word or from others. It was up to me. I had to fully trust in Him and once again drop everything I had on my agenda to follow His lead and watch

———

His plan unfold before me.

Only hours later, I began looking for plane tickets to Hong Kong. I felt peace about His request of me and knew in the depths of my heart that if I stepped forward in obedience, He would heal my back, align my finances and guide the way, just like He had done so many times before. I kept reminding myself that God is yesterday, today and forever the same, and if I did choose to put my full trust in Him, He would surely supply all of my needs.

After finding and purchasing a ticket for a flight leaving only a few weeks later, I resigned from my job with no intent to return. I didn't know how long this mission adventure would take. All I knew was that I would need to be back in time for Stephanie and me to travel to her home in Texas for our wedding. A feeling of relief consumed me, and a thrill of excitement started building inside as I counted down the days to departure. I found myself wondering why God had told me to go back to China and what He had in store for me there. I sought clues, but it quickly became apparent that He was not giving any.

———

Chapter Two

MY DEPARTURE WAS only a few days away, and I was still in immense pain and unable to lift my loaded backpack. The mere thought of how badly it was going to hurt to pick up that fifty-pound pack made me shudder. Once again, doubts assailed me. Was this really such a good idea? Did I actually hear from God that I was supposed to quit my job? I kept second-guessing my decision to obey what I thought I had been instructed to do. Returning to Scripture, I found comfort and relief in knowing that His ways and thoughts are higher than mine, and He kept reminding me of all the exciting miracles He had performed before my eyes in India, Bangladesh, Nepal and China on my previous trip. It seemed like yesterday, and I still remembered the child-like faith I had every time I prayed for someone with a severe medical condition they trusted God to take care of. God intervened and did exactly what He promised to do for His disciples as He shared the Great Commission with them. What bothered me in the present was why He did not intervene and heal me, even after I had so diligently moved forward in faith at His command.

The day finally came for me to travel to Oslo and board my plane to Hong Kong. I woke up to the sound of my alarm clock, too excited to remember to carefully roll out of bed like I had gotten accustomed to doing over the previous three months. I jumped out of my bed like a child getting up on Christmas morning and discovered in that very moment that my back pain was gone. Completely gone! I lifted the backpack off the floor in a swift motion to make sure my mind was not playing tricks on me. Again, no pain! The previous night, I would have groaned in agony because of my sudden move out of bed; now, I was completely pain free and healed. I found myself laughing and crying tears of joy all at the same time as I walked down the stairs with the fully loaded backpack on my back. I rushed into the kitchen to share the great news with my parents.

I was so excited about the amazing things God had in

store for me, and this miracle was confirmation to me that I had correctly moved in faith to follow His command. Even the uncomfortable, old-fashioned backpack felt comfortable in comparison to the nightmare of pain I had gone through leading up to this day.

My fiancée had already left for Thailand and was off to her mission adventure together with a small group of young adults from several nations. I missed her more than words could express, as I was unable to speak with her every day like we had been accustomed to doing. However, I knew she was in God's hands and that He would provide for her, protect her and lead her—just like He was going to do me.

As I boarded my flight for Asia, I felt goose bumps as I realized the trip was actually happening. The dreadfully long and cold winter months of pain in Sauda had passed, and God had brought me into a new spring season of adventure and excitement. I settled into my seat and quickly got into a great conversation with the gentleman sitting next to me. He eventually asked me where I was headed, and I had the opportunity to share my testimony of God's amazing love and the exciting life He has in store for those who put their full trust in Him.

———

As I shook that man's hand when we landed in Hong Kong, I was left with a certainty that the seeds sown through our conversation would at some point in the future flourish and bring him to a place of trusting Christ as His Savior. This was only the first of many divine appointments I encountered over the following weeks. A divine appointment is when God orchestrates someone crossing paths with you either to minister to you or for you to minister to them in some way. After my years on the mission field, I found that these divine appointments could take place at any point in time, and the only thing I needed to do to experience them was to hand over my day to God every morning. By surrendering my agenda and following His, I allowed Him to use me despite my shortcomings and lack of education and experience. If you desire to make a difference in people's lives, all God is looking for is a believer's willing heart to serve Him and love people.

Arriving at the mission base where I had previously served for two years was both magical and nostalgic. It felt as if I had reentered the closet leaving Narnia and that time had stood still while I had been gone. The leaders of the mission base embraced me and welcomed me back before finding me

———

a place to sleep. Missionaries from all over the world had come and gone after I had left, but many of my dear friends were still working on the base or in various places around mainland China, and I could not wait to see them again. I spent the next couple of days just catching up with old friends and sharing stories of God's goodness in our lives.

A couple of programs were going on at the base when I arrived, and a lot of new students from nations around the world had gathered together with one common goal—to spread the good news to the lost. Many of my old friends were now in leadership positions, and it brought joy to my heart to see the ripple effects of what God had done in their hearts while we had been out in the field together now affecting dozens of young lives as they were exposed to missionary life in Asia for the first time.

The mission base is located in the oldest part of Hong Kong, a 900-year-old village surrounded by ancestral worship temples. The narrow streets between the tall houses make you feel like you have stepped back in time and also serve as a strong contrast to the busy and crowded streets of Hong Kong with its population of 7.5 million people. Although there are severe strongholds of demonic powers throughout the village because of the idol worship and captivity its inhabitants are under, the mission base is a vibrant breath of fresh air in the center of the village where the sound of worship goes up to God's throne several times a day.

One of the neat things about the houses in this village and many other villages in the outskirts of Hong Kong is that there is usually a deck on top of each of the three- to four-story houses. From the flat roof deck, it's possible to overlook the village and all of its temples. In the distance you can see rice fields and a large grass-covered mountain as well as the skyscrapers of Yuen Long, a part of New Territories Hong Kong. The roof decks are not only remarkable in the sense that you have a 360-degree view of the surrounding areas, but they also serve as a perfect place for students and leaders to spend time with God and have their daily quiet time. As a result of the prayer blanket that was laid over these decks every morning, I was always struck and amazed by God's presence after climbing all the stairs to get to the roof. I knew this would be the perfect place for me to seek God's guidance about where I should go next. I had been obedient so far, dropping everything to come to Hong Kong; now I needed to find out where my adventure would take me from here.

I prayed, worshipped and sought God's presence for His guidance, but I heard nothing. He encouraged me and spoke to me through His Word like He does every day, but no still, small voice gave me guidance about the future. However, I remained confident that God would speak to me in His time; He had said He would, and I had already traveled half way around the world with a healed back, so I had every confidence that He would certainly not fail me now.

I spent the rest of my day getting to know some of the new students on the base that I had not met before, and to my great surprise I ran into a fellow Norwegian. He had just come to Hong Kong and was part of a discipleship training school program there as He felt that God had called him to minster in China. Little did either of us know at the time that, eleven years later, he and his future American wife would host my family and me as we traveled through China with our three children to explore ministry opportunities. It is really exciting to see how God works through relationships and to realize that He sees the future as if it were today. Never underestimate the opportunities God puts before you, big or small, as they may have ripple effects into your future in ways you could never imagine at the time. Walk in obedience and serve Him with excellence, and when you live in His will, your journey will be like putting together a puzzle with thousands of pieces when you are handed only a few pieces at a time. When you look back, you will see how the pieces fit together to create a beautiful masterpiece that only God Himself could have created. The picture will be used as a testimony to your children, your family and any other individual with whom you are willing to share it during your time here on earth.

The next morning I went back up to the roof deck, and the same thing happened. I sought God for guidance, but nothing came to me. I worshipped my heart out together with my new friend from Norway while gazing off to the mountains in the distance. All of a sudden, I was reminded of Psalms 121— "Where does my help come from?" I felt strongly impressed that I was to climb the mountain and seek God for direction there.

Later that same day, a couple of my friends and I hiked the mountain together. To reach our destination, we had to walk through several miles of narrow pavement paths leading through rice fields and fish farms. Getting out of the city and hearing the sounds of nature often brings a tranquility that

———

clears the mind and enables you to more clearly hear what the Lord wants to tell you. However, despite our half-day trip up to the peak, I received no additional direction after seeking God together with my friends on the mountaintop. What He did give me was a breath of fresh air and a gorgeous experience of His beautiful creation.

I didn't realize it, but God was preparing me for being persistent about pushing into His presence and being one hundred percent reliant on Him and His guidance. At the same time, He was also stirring up a fire in my heart about getting back into China and walking into His masterpiece of a mission adventure that He had prepared for me. As I stood there on the summit looking over the majestic city of Hong Kong on one side and the border to mainland China on the other, I started shedding tears of gratitude to God for bringing me back. I thanked Him for once again softening my heart for ministry and making my heart and mind a pipeline for His miracle-working power. In that moment, I felt closer to God than I had in months, and I was confident His guidance was right around the corner. As I started the descent with my friends, I felt a divine burst of energy fill me from within. I was ready!

———

Chapter Three

THE THIRD DAY after my arrival in Hong Kong, as I sat in a red recliner on the dormitory rooftop, God finally revealed my destination in China. I was literally through the roof with excitement. Finally! I remember that moment as clearly as if it were yesterday. I sat pleading with God for what seemed to be the hundredth time, "Where do You want me to go?" All of a sudden, He dropped seven letters into my mind which named a place I had never heard of and could never have come up with on my own. Bam! There it was! I hurriedly wrote it down in my journal exactly as I saw it in my mind before it slipped away: Xinlien.

I rushed down to the office and asked the mission base secretary for a map of China so I could locate the city or province where God wanted me to go. This was, of course,

———

before smart phones and Google Maps, so I was soon running back up the stairs with a thick hundred-page book that contained detailed maps of each of the Chinese provinces. I plopped back into the red recliner and opened the book like a child opening his first gift on Christmas morning. This was it!

The first map showed the entire country of China, but after several minutes of searching, I found nothing that resembled my word. Assuming it must not be a major city, I moved on to the individual province maps. I quickly scanned the maps, one after another, with eager eyes to find names starting with "X-i-n." I found a few, but with different endings. Did I get it wrong, God? Did I misspell it? Did I just want to hear You so badly that I made up a random Chinese word in my mind on my own? No, I refuse to believe that!

I took at deep breath and flipped another page when a sudden thought struck me. How could I be so stupid? Obviously, the city would be listed in the index in the back of the map book if it existed! While giving myself a mental slap in the face, I flipped to the very back of the book and found the page listing cities starting with the letter X. My heart sank as I noticed that there was no "Xinlien" listed. I slammed the

———

———

book closed and threw it on the table in front of me.

Finally, after three long days of seeking God, I had heard His voice...but now I was almost convinced that what I had heard was not from Him after all. For a moment, I was upset with God. Did You really bring me all this way just to sit around on a rooftop day in and day out? Am I even supposed to be here?

My thoughts quickly went back to Sauda, Norway, where less than one week earlier I had been lying on my bed in excruciating pain wondering fearfully how I could possibly carry my fully loaded backpack to and from an airport and travel to the other side of the world. In that moment, God told me, "Take a closer look!" I didn't know what to believe any more, but I picked up the map book from the table and flipped the pages to the first province, Anhui. I noticed the detailed map had hundreds of cities listed, some in block letters and other in very small writing. I assumed those in smaller print were considered small villages in comparison to the block-lettered cities. It took a few minutes to check all the cities, but none were the name I was looking for. Next!

I flipped the page to the next map, Fujian, and searched

———

the city listing diligently. Nothing! My excitement over hearing God's voice tell me to take a closer look started diminishing as I flipped one page after another. I am sure I sat hunched over that map in deep concentration for several hours. My head even started hurting from focusing so intently on the maps and small print.

As I began carefully looking over the map of the twenty-third (and last) Chinese province of Zhejiang, only a sliver of hope remained that I would find Xinlien. Sure enough, I once again found nothing! If I have learned anything during my twenty-two-year walk with Christ, it is that He will always find ways to stretch your patience and ability to get you out of your comfort zone. I was definitely not comfortable at this point; I was frustrated and desperate for guidance and about ready to call it a day. It was not even noon yet, and I felt like I had been studying maps all day. What now, God?

I took another deep breath, flipped the page and saw on the top of the next page in bold letters, "Autonomous Regions." Apparently China had five additional regions that were not considered provinces, and Tibet was probably the only one I had heard of before. On all of my previous trips to mainland China, I had traveled throughout the more common provinces in the south, but most of these autonomous regions were far away in the far west or north side of this massively long country. With renewed hope, I flipped the page and looked through the Guanxi map—nothing. I took a deep breath, then moved on to the Inner Mongolia map—nothing. Then Ningxia, but nothing. Then on to the second to the last map in the book, Xinjiang. The first thought that struck me as I looked at the map was, WOW! That region is humongous, covering the entire northwestern part of China, bordering Mongolia, Russia, Kazakhstan, Kyrgyzstan, Tajikistan, Afghanistan, Pakistan and India. Thankfully the 1.66 million square kilometer autonomous region seemed pretty densely populated, and my eyes glanced over the map in one last attempt to find my destination city, Xinlien. Please, God, please let this be it! My eyes glanced left and right on the map in search of cities starting with X.

Finally, there it was! Xinlien was located about as far northeast as you can possibly get in China, in a deep valley between two long mountains stretching from Kazakhstan and Kyrgyzstan. Ha! Here I had traveled from a small and seemingly insignificant town deep in a long fjord in Norway, only to find out that my destination is deep in a long Chinese

———

valley in the middle of nowhere. I chuckled to myself as I once again studied the tiny print reading Xinlien. It probably had the smallest print out of all the cities on the map, so I assumed it was a pretty small village or city. Nevertheless, the wait was over! The feeling of relief, excitement and joy was overflowing in my heart—I had to praise God, I had to tell someone! I bounced out of the recliner and rushed off to share the news with my friends. While running down the stairs, three steps at a time, I wondered how on earth I was going to get there? Before I had a chance to think, God spoke in my heart and told me, "I will lead the way!"

———

Chapter Four

I ASKED AROUND the base, one person after another. None of them had been to Xinjiang—much less Xinlien—not even the leaders who had been at the mission base for twenty years since most of their work had been centered in the southern part of the country. I went to a nearby Internet cafe (yes, those were the days) and tried to research Xinlien on the Internet, but I could find no information about this city. This was 2002, and although the Internet was up and running, it was definitely not providing information on just about anything imaginable like it is today. I was pretty much at a standstill. God was quiet, and I could find nothing useful to do to move in the right direction as He was waiting for me to move in faith.

I knew from experience in my walk with Christ that I

should not rush ahead of myself and act without having peace about my next step. His agenda and His plan is a masterpiece, and it is crucial to listen and seek His guidance to make sure my path aligns with His. After praying some more and talking to the base leaders, I was convinced that I was to join a large group of students and leaders who were about to travel to a Cultural Exchange program in Zhangjiajie in Hunan province. This move would at least get me into China and serve as a step in the right direction. I figured that my next clue would come from a divine appointment, someone who could tell me about this place and serve as a natural connection for me to go there.

The only challenge at this point was in fact that the group was leaving in only three days, and I needed to get my Chinese visa processed and accepted before then. The base leader was actually headed in with some other applications that very day, but he told me he could wait until first thing the next morning to allow me time to get my application completed so he could include it. That would, however, be my last chance to get my visa processed in time for departure. "All I need from you is three passport pictures, a completed application form and the fee for the visa, and I will take it in for you." I got the application and fee taken care of right away, but I had no passport pictures with me in my luggage from Norway. Being rushed for time, I asked George where I would need to go in Hong Kong to get pictures taken, and he told me a couple of different locations about an hour away by bus. It was already past noon when I took off on the local bus from the ancient Chinese village where the base was located, headed for the big city. If you have never been to Hong Kong, it is a megacity with about seven million people and probably as many signs in Cantonese overhanging the sides of the crowded streets. Skyscrapers, trains, buses, taxis, cars and millions of locals fill the streets every day, creating a somewhat confusing setting for a Norwegian searching for a shop to get my passport pictures taken. The only positive is that I was about a head taller than most everyone else walking down the streets; unfortunately, that didn't help me interpret the signs. An afternoon of frustration and confusion passed by quickly as I was unsuccessful in locating the place George had told me to find. I had no cell phone with Google maps or a GPS at the time, and eventually I had to jump on a bus back to the village and let George know that I would likely not be able to join the group entering China as planned. With my head hanging low, I got off the bus and navigated through the narrow back alleys of the ancient village leading to the mission base on autopilot.

I can honestly say my heart stopped for at least a few seconds as I suddenly walked up on a giant, bewildered water buffalo that had wandered into the back alleys from the nearby fields. The shock of looking into the eyes of the confused thousand-pound animal and seeing it bolt and trot away down the street very efficiently helped me snap out of my slump. "Wow, that was intense!" I laughed to myself as I lifted my head high and walked upright back to the mission base. God has always been and will always be faithful, so I muttered to myself as I kept on walking, "You've got this, God. You will work this out in my favor despite my circumstances! If it is Your will for me to join the group to Zhangjiajie, You will make it happen."

It was dark outside by the time I opened the large black iron gate to the front yard of the mission base and walked up the stairway, dodging hundreds of colorful bugs circling the lamps. I opened the door to the dormitory and walked over to the bedroom where I had been sleeping for the last week since I arrived Hong Kong. I flipped the light switch and noticed an envelope lying on my pillow. I rushed over to the bed, picked it up and opened it and just about lost my breath in awe as I saw what was inside. Inside the envelope was a handwritten note from one of my friends who worked at the mission base office. "Look what we found in our office today, probably left behind from last year!" Behind the note were three passport pictures—exactly what I needed to give to George that night to go with my visa application so he could get it approved the next morning. I began to laugh with joy over how incredible it was that God really does pay attention to the little details of our everyday lives, if we surrender them to Him. More often than not, He wants to bring us to a place where only He can solve our situation before the miracle happens before our very eyes. The sooner we surrender to His will and get on His agenda, the more efficiently He can step in and do amazing things.

I sure slept well that night, knowing that everything was going to work out and that I was only a couple of days away from entering the great land of China again. God was in control, and He had prepared the way for me. He never said walking in faith would be easy, but it sure is rewarding as every demonstration of His intervention roared of His love

———

and care for me.

Chapter Five

I HAD VISITED the Zhangjiajie program twice before a couple of years back and seen several university students come to faith through this really neat cultural exchange program that lasted for about two weeks. The idea behind the program was for the participants to attend various introductory classes on Chinese language, arts, culture and music and then for the university students to have the opportunity to practice their English skills with the team members as we circulated around the campus. Every so often they had an "English Corner" where Chinese students showed up at a certain location on the campus, eager to practice their English skills with each other. The attendance to these English Corners always skyrocketed when there were actual English-speaking people attending from other

———

countries. The setup couldn't be more perfect for friendship evangelism as we were able to build friendships with these Chinese students who were wide open to learning about our culture, language, background and faith. The only way I would describe a non-Christian young adult in this part of China would be as a wide-open book with blank pages. They are eager to understand and have very few pre-conceived ideas about what the Christian faith is all about. Apart from briefly being told the Gospel story in the format of a fairy tale, they are taught to believe in nothing and strive to make their way through life in their own power. Chinese children and young adults are typically much more motivated to succeed academically than what I have found to be the case in other places in the world, especially in my home country. If we are to make an impact coming in from the outside with the Gospel, it is particularly through raising up fearless disciples of this young generation that can bring the truth to their own people without having to jump the hurdles of communication, social or cultural barriers.

A year earlier while participating in the same cultural exchange program, I had built a strong friendship with one specific Chinese student, about nineteen years of age. For his

———

protection, we will call him Luke. Jesse, a good friend of mine, and I ministered to him and shared the simplified Gospel story followed by using some very powerful evangelism tools that show how common Biblical stories from Genesis are found in the complex Chinese character system. He was utterly amazed at the connection between the Bible and his very own written language and showed great interest in the Gospel story; however, he never took a stand for Christ during our stay there. When it was time for us to leave, we left him a pocket-sized Chinese Bible and prayed God would keep working on his heart.

Now, as I headed back to the same campus, my dear friend Jesse, who I had ministered together with a year ago, just so happened to travel together with me as part of the group. A day or so after we arrived at the university, we saw Luke running up to us with excitement in his eyes. After giving my friend and me a great big hug, he pulled his Bible out of one jacket pocket and a notebook out of the other and eagerly asked us to sit down. As his eyes filled with tears, he opened his notebook and showed us that it was full, front to back, of questions he had written down as he had studied through the Bible we had given him several times over the last

TO THE ENDS OF THE EARTH

twelve months. He looked deep into my eyes and pleaded desperately: "I need you to answer these questions for me; I can't understand it all. I have been waiting for you to come back to help me!" We walked him through all the questions and ministered to him through the answers, and when we got to the last page, he told us with a great big smile on his face and tears streaming down his face, "I want to become a Christian. I believe Jesus died for me!"

This was without a doubt another divine appointment lined up specifically for this trip. I was simply blown away by the way God had worked through His Holy Spirit in Luke's life while we had been gone. All we needed to do was show up, explain the Gospel one more time and then lead Him to Christ. It still moves my heart and brings me to tears fifteen years later when I think about Luke and the fact that he is today leading a large ministry in reaching out to his own minority people group. Over the last few years, he has taken numerous teams of Chinese pioneer missionaries that he has led to salvation and discipled into isolated villages of his own unreached minority people group. As they work to reach one village at a time, they are ultimately reaching this people group for Christ. You never know the ripple effects that will occur when you step forward in obedience and let God use you through divine appointments to share the Gospel with individuals that cross your path. Sixteen years ago, we met this young nineteen year old who had never heard about Christ before; we sowed seeds of faith through speaking the truth and left him with a Bible. God used His Word to pull Luke close and, when we crossed his path again a year later, he was ripe and ready to start his own journey with Christ. It blows my mind that this meeting was the birth of a movement that is reaching an unreached people group with the Gospel.

Chapter Six

GOD WASN'T FINISHED yet; I was still to encounter several more divine appointments that would steer me towards Xinlien, at this point 2,500 miles away from where I was located. A few days later, a missionary from Singapore just happened to stop by the university to speak to our group at the campus hotel where we were staying. After an amazing a cappella worship session that brought me to tears due to God's goodness and wondrous works, Jacob from Singapore raised his voice, introduced himself and shared stories about his ministry that was located only a few hours away. He was a very soft-spoken man in his thirties at the time, but with an uncommon heart for God and for children. It is a joy to my heart to know that this man leads a major organization today that ministers to a portion of the sixty-one million "left-behind" children in China today.

After the evening meeting, I got into a long conversation with Jacob, and he wanted to hear my story. After mentioning that God had told me to go to Xinlien in the autonomous region of Xinjiang, his eyes popped open. He had some friends that happened to work in the capital city of that region, Urumqi. He had also heard through those friends of a Norwegian-American couple that worked at a university there. After corresponding with his friend by e-mail, he found out the name of the university but could not seem to find the name of the couple apart from their nationalities. Jacob said he was sorry for not being able to retrieve any more information for me, but thought I would be able to locate them if I went to the university and looked for them. I was overwhelmed with gratitude that Jacob had crossed my path, and that he had provided me with a link that might be able to get me to Xinlien. However, the blessing didn't end there. Before taking off to go back to his home city, Jacob gave me his address and contact information and told me that there were flights going directly to Urumqi from his city. He also said he would be happy to have me stay at his house while he helped me find plane tickets. I couldn't believe it! I knew

God worked in mysterious ways, but this was just too much to be a coincidence.

The next week was unbelievable. Knowing that God had made a way for me to continue my journey towards Xinlien enabled me to focus and make the most of the last few days in the cultural exchange program. Who knows what the ripple effects have been from the many individuals that heard the Gospel for the first time during those days. Some came to faith there and then, and we left others, as we had Luke a year earlier, with a Bible in hand and a hunger to seek answers.

One aspect of working in this type of ministry is that we always had to remain aware that a governmental investigation bureau was keeping an eye on us. It was not uncommon to see black cars parked by the road close to where we were staying and agents keeping an eye on us as we moved between the university campus and various outing locations. China has historically been very much closed to religious influence, and the government is very critical of westerners coming in to present their faith to the locals. For that reason, you would never find any one of us speaking up about Christ in public or preaching to a crowd. All evangelism took place one on one through the natural process of relationship building, which is in my opinion the best way to communicate the Gospel anyway. The power of your testimony and communicating the way Christ has changed your life, from your heart to the heart of a non-believer, can often be more powerful than hearing a sermon from a stranger on television or from a pulpit. The Holy Spirit works through His people, and that is why it is so crucial for us to allow Him to speak through us to the lost and needy. We are His body on earth, and if we are all relying on the pulpit preachers to do the task of spreading His Gospel of love, we have missed the target of the Great Commission. I cannot emphasize enough the fact that God is searching for a willing heart, for the ones willing to lay down their own heart to have Him speak through them. You don't have to present God with a list of qualifications or a degree from a seminary or Bible school; if you have received Christ as your Savior, you are already a testimony of His salvation power to the world. Your testimony has the power to lead other people to the same place. Share it!

Chapter Seven

GOD SPEAKS IN multiple ways, but I have found one common denominator in being able to clearly hear what He wants to tell me: eliminate all distractions and put all your focus on Him. He is not somewhere far away waiting for you to call out His name; He is right in your heart by His Holy Spirit if You have invited Him into your life. In our fast-paced, modern-day world, we strive to make everything time efficient and practical to enable us to accomplish more. As a result, our level of patience suffers. When praying to God, we very often have to be patient as His answer will come in His time. He knows every heart and every story of everyone on our planet, and it is certainly safe to say that He knows better than we do the implications of His divine interventions.

———

My favorite place to hear God's voice is in nature—on a mountaintop or a forest path or an open plain. Nature and creation alone speak loud and clear about His masterpiece and how much He loves us, but I have also found that as nature helps me still my heart and thoughts, God speaks to me through His still, small voice in my heart. Try it for yourself; I promise you He will not let you down if you are patient with Him. At first you will think that you are hearing your own thoughts speak what you want to hear; but then, as He speaks exactly what you need to hear again and again, you will start to recognize His voice. You will also find that, as you study His Word and memorize His promises, He will bring them to your attention at the times when you need them.

This particular morning I was out for an early morning walk on a nature trail that circled the university campus. It didn't take long before I found myself begging God to do something miraculous. The last few days had stirred my heart for the lost, for all the students that had never heard about Jesus and the fullness of life that can be experienced as you allow Him to be first in your life. I prayed for all the students that we had seen come to salvation over the last few days, that they would hear God's voice and guidance in their lives and

———

be able to connect with each other to support each other in prayer and fellowship against the attacks of the enemy. I then started praying for a breakthrough. I proclaimed that today one more person would come to know Jesus as Savior. God quickly spoke to me, "Believe for more!" I proclaimed out loud; "TWO. Jesus, bring two students to You through the ministry of our team today!"

By the time I was praying this prayer, the nature trail had brought me to an opening in the forest with a panoramic view overlooking all the student dorms at the university. I kept praying and believing as my heart was aching to see more people come to know God's unmatched love and freedom. The calm prayers turned into proclamations, then to worship and finally to me rebuking the evil one for the strongholds that he had formed over this area and the students. It was one of the most powerful prayer walks I had ever experienced as God kept building my faith as I declared His truth and His breakthrough on the campus. Before I walked back to the group, I told God, "More than TWO. I believe You will bring more than two individuals to salvation today!"

That day went on as what I would at this point refer to as "normal," one divine appointment after another, giving us opportunities left and right to share the Gospel with Chinese students who had never heard about Jesus before. By suppertime, Jesse came running up to me with the biggest smile on his face. He eagerly whispered to me that he had some really exciting news to share with me. He had hung out with Luke that morning and, before he knew it, Luke was sharing his testimony with his best friend, Xi. Luke shared his story passionately in his own local language to his friend who was from the same unreached minority group. A few minutes later, Luke looked over at Jesse and asked him if he could lead Xi in the salvation prayer, just like we had done with him a couple of days before. Jesse taught Luke how to lead someone to salvation, and then Luke helped his friend pray the prayer in his own language!

Jesse stopped to take a small swallow of the hot green tea that had been poured before him at the round dining room table, before he continued sharing the story with me as quietly as he could. One of the main reasons the Chinese students got radically engaged in sharing the Gospel with their friends was the fact that we showed them how to hear God's voice right off the bat. We shared that God is a personal God, their Father, their Creator, who wants to have a personal relationship with them. We taught them that if you quiet yourself down to truly listen for His direction, He will speak to you in many different ways.

More often than not, we saw our new brothers and sisters in Christ hear His still, small voice in their own mother tongue very quickly after receiving salvation. Luke's friend was not an exception, and he was quick to respond to God's voice when he was told to go get his girlfriend and share the Gospel with her too.

A few minutes later Jesse, Luke and Xi headed over to the building where Xi's girlfriend was and started sharing their testimony with her. Not long after, she bowed her head and received Christ. As if that were not enough, later that day, another friend of Xi's was led to salvation. Jesse told me he had never seen such a chain of events leading to so many being saved at once; he was blown away that he had been given the opportunity to witness such a great blessing from God.

The stories from my stay in Zhangjiajie alone would be enough to fill this book, but my journey to Xinlien had only just begun and my time in Zhangjiajie had come to an end for the present. The program concluded with a great trip to the Zhangjiajie National Forest Park, a place of mountain pillar formations so magnificent and spectacular that words cannot do it justice. If you have ever watched the movie Avatar, the scenes with the floating mountains could have been taken straight out of this national park as its tall, narrow pillars seem to defy gravity.   God has blessed me with the opportunity to travel throughout many different nations during my years in full-time ministry, and every single country I have visited is unique and beautiful in its own way. When people ask for evidence of God's existence, I always want to jump out of my seat, raise my voice and say, "Look around you!" The fact that we are even able to see the incredibly beautiful creation all around us is evidence of a Creator. Your body, cells, molecules and atoms are all proclaiming the fact that there is a perfect Creator who created us in His image.

If you don't believe in miracles, you need to understand that you are a walking miracle with a unique DNA that is unlike anybody else on the planet—from the smallest atom to the end of our solar system, which is one of an unlimited number of solar systems in an unlimited number of galaxies in an unlimited number of clusters and super-clusters of

———

galaxies—if this is not evidence of God's creation, I don't know what is.

Our God's creation is all around us and in us, and it is incomprehensible and endless, just like God's everlasting love for His children, for you and me. Realizing and personally experiencing that the Creator of the universe cared enough about me to speak directly into my heart about what I should do in my everyday life to best share His love to others blows my mind. I welcome you to allow it to blow yours as well.

———

Chapter Eight

AFTER A TRAIN trip to the nearby city where Jacob and his beautiful little family lived, I got in touch with him by phone and found my way to his apartment. The few days I spent with Jacob were short but very valuable for the rest of my mission adventure. He prepared me for what I might possibly be facing in the next stages of my trip. After buying a plane ticket to Urumqi, Xinjiang, we created a list of essentials I needed for the remainder of my journey. He strongly suggested I get a tent, sleeping bag and survival equipment should I ever have to camp under the open sky. Since I was traveling north, I needed to be prepared for temperatures that would drop well below freezing at night. He generously helped me repack my dad's old green backpack, and what he didn't already have at his house to give me, we

———

purchased before my departure. I was so grateful that God had sent Jacob to cross paths with me so that I could listen to his valuable input about what I could expect in the region where I was headed.

Taking flights within China was certainly nothing like going through international airports. Nobody seemed to speak or understand English. From this point forward, I had to communicate using the little bit of Chinese I had learned over the previous two to three years and the help of my dictionary and Mandarin phrase book. I was no longer with a team, and I had no English-speaking contact. All I had at this point was a paper in my pocket with the name of an Urumqi university written in Chinese characters.

For some reason, despite all these limitations, I didn't have a single worry. I felt God had perfectly orchestrated my trip thus far, and He was surely not going to leave me now. As I continued my journey towards Xinlien, I felt certain I was safe in His will and that He had gone before me, orchestrating my way. As I boarded the airplane and found my seat, I felt God's comforting peace come over me. He had already prepared the way for me; all I needed to do was keep my heart connection with Him and stay in His will every

———

single day.

The flight from Hunan to Urumqi was memorable. I remember sitting by the window and watching the terrain rapidly change as we flew over Tibet and entered the gigantic Xinjiang region. It felt like I had entered an entirely different country. The rice fields and tropical forests were replaced with jagged mountain formations and grass-covered hills as far as the eye could see. The mountains reminded me of when I had traveled through the foothills of the Himalayas in Nepal a couple of years earlier, and as I took in the majestically beautiful sights, I felt a renewed strength and excitement for the continuation of my journey.

I arrived at the airport late at night and asked the first taxi driver I saw to take me to the closest hotel. Unfortunately I did not know how to express my wish to go to an inexpensive hotel, so I ended up at a five-star luxury resort. As it was eleven o'clock at night, there was nothing left for me to do but pay the money and enjoy the luxury God had put before me. I probably slept better that night than on any other night of my trip, but when morning came, I was again faced with the reality of my adventure.

———

I pulled out the handwritten note with the university name and started wondering how I would find the international couple that lived there. I didn't even know if they still lived or worked there, but if God had laid this puzzle piece in my hand, I was certain there was a reason. As doubt began to enter my mind, I reached for my Bible and God's incredible peace flowed into my heart as I read His countless promises to me.

After a rejuvenating morning devotion and a delicious Chinese hotel breakfast, I walked outside, found a cab and showed the driver the name of the university Jacob had written down for me a week and a half before. As we started driving, I quickly realized Urumqi was a very large city with numerous skyscrapers and that it was a whole lot cooler than I had expected. Riding in the backseat of the taxi with the windows rolled half way down, I quickly wished I had put on a few more layers of clothes. About forty-five minutes later, we pulled up at the entrance of a large campus. The sign by the gated entrance matched the Chinese characters on the paper I had shown the driver, so I paid the fare, thanked him for the ride, slung my backpack over my shoulder and got out of the car.

———

——————

This is it, God! Now it is up to You! I was standing before a campus with probably thousands of students and hundreds of staff members, and dozens of dorms and campus buildings as far as I could see. I gave the moment to God and asked Him to guide my steps. After a few minutes of walking down a street with campus dorms and apartment buildings on both sides, I felt the Holy Spirit told me to stop and request help from a local student coming out of one of the doors. Knowing I had to seize the moment, I hurried up to him and told him I was looking for an American-Norwegian couple living somewhere on the campus. The answer just about knocked me to the ground: "Yes, sir, of course. Their apartment is right up here on the third floor. Here, let me hold the door for you." Still shaking from this undeniable guidance of the Holy Spirit, I halfway sprinted up the three flights of stairs and found the apartment door. I rang the doorbell and thirty seconds later found myself sharing my entire story up until that point in my native language to a fellow Norwegian. We were both amazed at God's goodness and guidance as I wrapped up the story with the four words, "and here I am!"

The couple, Sara and John, and their two children had the biggest smiles on their faces as they invited me into their

——————

apartment. They quickly made up one of the kid's rooms into a guest room and whipped up a delicious meal. We spent the rest of the evening getting to know each other and sharing testimonies of how God was moving in the country. They told me that I could stay as their guest as long as I needed until God revealed the next connection that would lead me closer to my destination. They didn't personally know anything about the place I wanted to go and they didn't know anyone who did, but they were sure God would send the right person my way soon.

It was amazing to hear their own story of how they had moved to this town as "tentmakers" in obedience to their calling, and were now raising their two small children while also teaching at the university. They were part of a large network of foreigners working in the capital city and just so happened to have plans to attend a gathering a few days later. I was of course strongly encouraged to join them, as my next connection could be a part of this group.

Every single morning I got up and dove into God's Word seeking His guidance and asking Him to fill me up for what lay ahead of me. I knew I wasn't being led to Xinlien just to visit; something bigger was in the works, and I wanted to be spiritually ready for any challenge that came my way. I also prayed earnestly for my fiancée to have a life-changing time in Thailand. Every evening I would write a few pages in my journal to her about what God was doing and how my heart was aching to see her again. Little did I know as I was writing this journal that my words would serve as a way for me to put pen to paper and write this book sixteen years later.

The third day after arriving at the apartment, Sara came up to me before breakfast and asked if I would like to come with them as they were running some errands around town after breakfast. She laughed as I replied that I wasn't sure because I hadn't yet asked God what was on His agenda for my day. I had never gone to this extreme in my walk with God before this point, but after three weeks of walking in daily obedience to His guidance and moving from one divine appointment to another, I was very focused on my need to stay fully on His agenda.

Looking back on that moment, I realize God is not expecting us to walk around like robots waiting for His next command, but that He desires a heart connection and personal relationship with us so that He can guide our walk and show us divine appointments as He longs to work through us. He has created in us a mind of our own which He wants to transform daily so that His thoughts can be our thoughts. He doesn't only want us to give Him five or ten minutes in the beginning of each day, He wants to be the center of our day, our week and essentially our lives. He wants to be the center of our decisions, victories, challenges, sorrows and joys. He wants to be the center of our family, our church, our workplace and most assuredly the navigator of our lives. His Holy Spirit can serve like a GPS that leads us to God's unique plan and purpose for our lives—lives lived to the fullest, full of joy and His power, living in His promises every single day. Every time we make a wrong turn and start heading away from this purpose, the Holy Spirit will want to guide us back to the route that perfectly aligns with God's Word and His heart.

That night I found myself in a crowded room of forty or so tentmakers from all over the world. I was fully expecting to find my next connection to Xinlien and tried to talk to as many people as possible to see if anyone knew anything about the town and how to get there. At the end of the meeting, I got into a conversation with a South Korean couple who had heard about the town and the valley in which it was located.

My heart sank as they told me that the area was closed to foreigners due to governmental projects going on in the area and that, as far as they knew, no foreigner had set foot in Xinlien for the last several decades.

The conversation left me with a heavy feeling of disappointment and confusion. Did God bring me all this way only to shut the door in my face when I was this close to my destination? If no other foreigner had been allowed access to the city for governmental reasons, how would a twenty-one-year-old Norwegian traveling on a tourist visa gain access without even knowing anyone in the area? The meeting ended and we went back to the apartment.

When my head hit the pillow that night, I cried out to God that I wanted Him to take the heaviness from me. I laid the disappointment on Him, closed my eyes and slept—but I woke the next day to the same feeling of disappointment. Before I had even gotten out of bed, my mind was filled with doubt and worry—and I was unable to shake the feeling. This time it seemed like the door had been slammed shut right in my face. We were no longer talking about just the need of finding a contact person and a means of transportation to take me to my destination. Now I was dealing with a governmental restriction on foreigners trying to enter the area. With the governmental investigation bureau tracking my every move, I wanted to be sure I didn't get into trouble to the point where they would arrest me or evict me from the country. As much as my heart was willing to be persecuted for my faith and mission, I didn't see how making an unwise move without direction would be God's will at this point.

The day passed slowly and, although John and Sara tried to encourage me that God had this, I was not convinced, not yet anyway. That night while drifting off to sleep, I was reminded of one of my mom's worship records from the Pensacola revival that she occasionally played during her morning quiet times back in Norway. Don Moen's lyrics, "God will make a way, where there seems to be no way. He works in ways we cannot see, He will make a way for me. He will be my guide, hold me closely to His side, with love and strength for each new day, He will make a way, He will make a way." That song could not have been more fitting to my situation. As I sang that song quietly to myself while falling asleep in God's presence, I felt a break in the spiritual atmosphere. Tomorrow, God would make a way.

Chapter Nine

I WOKE UP the next morning, had my time with God, ate breakfast and realized the heaviness was gone. I had now been with this family for almost a week, and I felt it was high time I got on with my journey. I kept praying under my breath, "Please, God, make a way for me today!"

A couple of hours later, Sara received an unexpected phone call from an old Chinese friend that they had led to Christ a couple of years earlier. He had moved from Urumqi a few months ago for family reasons, and they had lost contact with him and his wife, until now. I couldn't follow the conversation as she was speaking in Chinese, but I noticed how Sara's face lit up after only a couple of minutes and how she sounded very upbeat and excited as she conversed with this gentleman over the phone. The conversation went on for

———

about fifteen minutes before she gently placed her phone down on the table. She took a deep breath and then asked me if I was ready for some good news. For the next few minutes she told me the story about this young man who had attended one of the ministries in the city where he had come to faith in Christ. He had grown to become a strong believer and both he and his wife been John and Sara's close friends until they had moved away. At this point, John and Sara had not heard from the couple for over six months and had no idea where they had moved. The man, David, had called Sara that day from his wife's hometown, where they were spending the next few weeks because of some health issues with his mother-in-law. When Sara told me the name of the wife's hometown, I just about hit the floor—they were in Xinlien! I could not believe it!

David had told Sara that he had woken up that morning and God had put it on his heart to give Sara a call. He had no idea about the reason why or why it was so important to speak with her that specific day, but now we all knew why. David was obviously the final connection for me to get to Xinlien; but we still needed to know how I would get past the governmental restrictions in the area.

———

David thought he could find a way for me to enter and had told Sara that he would call her back that evening with details about how we could make it work. Sure enough, a few hours later, David called back and shared with Sara that his retired father-in-law had worked for the government for the last thirty years in one of the higher ranked positions in the municipality. His sister-in-law also owned the only hotel in the city. Although they were both unbelievers, his mother-in-law had recently become a Christian, and the family said they would help me gain access to come to town for a visit!

The significance of his sister-in-law owning a hotel was the fact that every hotel that hosts a foreigner has to report a copy of the visitor's passport to the government so they can track you and make sure you are staying within your boundaries. Because she owned the hotel, I would be able to stay in the area undocumented; the father-in-law also told David to go ahead and bring me into the city for a visit and that he would keep the government off my back.

This masterpiece of unlikely pieces would, amazingly enough, make me the first foreigner to arrive and stay in the city since the area had been locked down decades ago. Now, we just needed to figure out how I would get there. The next morning David called back with specific instructions for me to get a plane ticket and fly to Yining, also known as Ghulja, a city of about half a million people on the very border of Kazakhstan. He didn't want to meet me at the airport, as it was too public, so we agreed that I would meet him outside a local motel early in the morning the day after I flew in.

The instructions he gave us were reminiscent of spy movies, and it was very apparent that we needed to make sure we didn't give the Yining authorities any reason to suspect anything as we headed into the Xinlien territory. David told me to make sure I got a local backpack and to avoid wearing any clothes or items to indicate that I was a foreigner. His plan was to portray me as a Russian, as many Russian Chinese people lived in this area, and they have similar features to Scandinavians. With careful planning, he was certain we could make it past the authorities in Yining into Xinlien where it was somewhat safe for me to reside as long as I was under the protection of his wife's family.

Chapter Ten

THAT SAME DAY, John and I went to a travel agency in Urumqi and bought plane tickets for a couple of days later to Yining. In the meantime we were able to go to a local market and pick out a new backpack for me to replace my dad's thirty-year-old backpack. I closed my eyes and prayed my dad would forgive me as I left the backpack behind in Urumqi, but I could obviously not take any chances at this point of standing out any more than I already was. I also found myself a couple of outfits that matched what most Chinese men in the area would wear.

Wednesday evening, I picked up my English-Mandarin phrase book once again and took off on my own. The next twenty-four hours would be crucial to the success of this mission, and I was all on my own, with my limited ability to speak and understand Chinese. After a short one-hour flight in another small and crowded Chinese aircraft, I once again landed in an unknown city where I knew no one. Until I met David the next morning, I needed to figure out how to get to the motel and hopefully catch some sleep. A long taxi ride later, I found myself at a run-down motel which, by the looks of it, barely qualified for a single star. It was ten o'clock at night when I walked in and asked the receptionist for a room. The small lobby was filled with cigarette smoke, and I was not surprised to find that the desk clerk neither spoke nor understood a single word of English. I couldn't even grasp much of the man's Mandarin Chinese due to his very heavy dialect. Thankfully, he did understand me as I asked for a room for the night in Chinese. He led me up a dark stairway and down a narrow hallway to my room. When I entered the dark, shabby-looking room that reeked of cigarette smoke, I noticed there were two single beds but had no idea that I had been given the key to a shared room. With a grateful heart I walked into the room and put my backpack on the floor. Apart from the two beds, the room had a night table in the middle and a plastic chair by the window, which was wide open. I was glad the windows were open due to the intense cigarette smell; I hoped it would air out quickly so that I could rest well. The bed was rock hard like most other hotel beds in China, much like lying down on a piece of cardboard on a concrete floor. The Chinese have a long, deeply rooted belief that sleeping on anything soft will damage the spine and lead to spinal issues later in life. As a matter of fact, it is not uncommon to not even use pillows because Chinese people in general believe pillows will result in posture issues.

About half an hour after I went to bed and tried unsuccessfully to sleep, the door to my room swung open and my heart stopped for a brief moment. A drunk Chinese man in his mid fifties stumbled into the room and over to the empty single bed. He sat down on the edge of the bed and pulled out an unlabeled bottle and placed it on the bedside table. He said nothing, but emanated a strong, repulsive smell of alcohol that quickly made its way across the three-foot gap between the two beds in the room.

It occurred to me that I was in a large city only miles away from the Kazakhstan border in a run-down, dark, dirty half-star motel, now accompanied by a drunken stranger that hopefully had no intentions except to sleep it off for the night. I turned my back to the man, closed my eyes and spent a few

TO THE ENDS OF THE EARTH

minutes in prayer, asking God to ensure He was surrounding me with His angels for the night. I asked Him to protect me and keep me safe for the next few hours until my scheduled meeting with David at dawn next morning.

Remembering that stress-filled night, I have no idea if I got any sleep or not; but I do remember getting out of that motel fairly quickly the next morning. I ran down the stairs, thanked the receptionist for my "pleasant" stay and headed outside. I had David's cell phone number with me just in case, but I prayed and hoped he would be there right at the time we had agreed over the phone only a few days before. Of course I had no idea what David looked like, but I had been told he was in his late thirties and somewhat taller than the norm. A few minutes later, a man that I assumed to be David came walking around the corner of the motel. He calmly strolled over to me, nonchalantly shook my hand and told me to come with him as he kept on moving past me. I followed him around the other corner of the hotel and down a back alley. Very quietly, he whispered to me in English that he was in fact David and that he would be thrilled to get to know me better, when we could, but that it was important right now for us to move along while attracting as little notice as possible. David told me that we needed to walk from the hotel to the local bus terminal, and that he looked forward to talking more with me along the way.

Try to imagine the thrill of the situation as I found myself walking down a dark back alley in Yining, following a person I had never met before—the one individual that would make it possible for me to enter Xinlien, sent by God himself. I was literally walking in a master plan crafted by my Father in heaven, in a special mission to bring light to the darkness. Each piece to this puzzle was falling into place, one by one, and although I could not see the finished work at that moment, I knew it would be a beautiful masterpiece in the end. My heart was tuned to God's will, and because my agenda, ideas and expectations were not getting in the way, He was able to lead me according to His will alone.

Chapter Eleven

I AM CONFIDENT we all have a choice every single morning to tune in to God's will for our lives and allow Him to use us. It doesn't matter if you wake up in the comfort of your own soft bed at home, in a college dorm surrounded my non-believers or in a rock hard bed in a dingy motel in the heart of China next to a drunk Chinese stranger; God is there through His Holy Spirit. He is always ready to speak to you if you quiet down and let Him; He wants you to seek Him first; He wants to bless you with everything you need to live your life to the fullest.

After checking to be sure nobody was around as we walked down that back alley, David whispered in my ear that it was very important that I keep quiet during the next few hours. I could not reveal to anyone that I was a foreigner and needed to make sure I came across as a Russian local to everyone with whom we came in contact. As we continued walking, he pulled a black garbage bag out of his jacket pocket and covered up my backpack in a swift motion. He told me this was customary for locals in order to protect their backpacks, rice bags and suitcases from rain as they were usually stowed on top of the roof when traveling by bus. It would also help us avoid attention as we approached the bus stop. Only moments later, we entered the bus terminal and joined the crowd outside of an old, run-down bus that seemed to have seating for about twenty-five people. The crowd must have been closer to twice that number, so I was a bit nervous that we would have to wait for a later bus. However, I remembered David's directions about being quiet around other people, so I stayed in line and kept my head low to avoid making eye contact with anyone.

A few minutes later, the bus driver and his assistant climbed up on the roof of the bus and started receiving bags from the travelers eager to get going. David tossed his bag up to the driver and helped me lift my heavy backpack up to the driver as well. Thanks to the black garbage bag, there was no way to tell that I was probably the only traveler with a backpack as most of the other local travelers used rice bags. People started getting onto the bus, and I noticed how the locals crammed into the back of the bus first in a very orderly fashion; and for every two seats, you would find three Chinese people sitting side by side, as if they had never done it any other way. David and I were among the last ones to board. We sat down together with another local about two rows behind the driver, and off we went. The bus must have been at least as old as I was, and it undoubtedly had a good old diesel engine as you could barely hear anything above the sound of the engine as it pulled out of the bus terminal and headed down the highway.

Within fifteen minutes, we were outside of Yining in the middle of the countryside. Rice fields, farms and raw land stretched around us as far as the eye could see, and before long, the landscape changed from flat fields to rolling hills. Another couple of hours passed, and we began seeing mountains on each side of the road. The road had now evolved from being a somewhat nicely maintained road to a farm road that resembled a Swiss cheese due to the abundance of potholes. The bus driver seemed very familiar with the pattern, as he skillfully swerved around just about every single pothole that I could see from where I was sitting on the bus.

Unfortunately, one thing that our bus driver was not good at was making stops. There were no towns as far as the eye could see, so the bus kept on going. After three hours or so, I needed a restroom. I was hoping we were almost to Xinlien, but I had forgotten to ask David how long I could expect the ride to be. Three hours turned into four hours, and my bladder was about to burst. I looked at David and quietly said bathroom in Chinese. David immediately got out of his seat to get the bus driver's attention and asked if the bus could stop to allow him to use the restroom. I could hear a sigh of relief from several of the other passengers as the driver quickly pulled the bus over to the side of the road.

Going out the door together with a group of men, the beauty of the surrounding countryside hit me. The rolling hills went on for miles and miles, with no houses or farms in sight. Far off in the distance was an endless trail of gorgeous snow-covered mountains leading towards our destination, Xinlien.

I quickly ran behind a large tree for privacy in my

moment of agony. Unfortunately, I had waited so long that I was unable to go. Frustrated and in pain, I hurried back to the bus and was last to board. I for sure didn't want that bus to leave me behind, especially since there were no signs of civilization as far as the eye could see.

I gave David a polite nod to thank him for the gesture of having the bus pull over and got back in my seat, praying and hoping that we would arrive at our destination soon. Sure enough, about an hour later, we saw houses appear in the distance. The mountain ranges were now considerably closer on each side of the road, and the rolling hills reminded me of Switzerland as most of them had sharp inclines, all covered in bright green foot-long grass that blew in the wind. As I continued looking at the hills, I noticed little Chinese kids running up and down the hillsides, playing and laughing. Seeing their smiles and observing the flock of sheep that came walking over the hilltop served to distract me from my discomfort for the last twenty minutes of our journey.

Xinlien looked to be a small town, with only a couple of buildings that were more than two stories high. People were walking up and down the streets, like in any other Chinese town I had been to, and quite a few were riding bicycles right along with the cars on the single-lane road that led up to the bus terminal. I was one of the first people off the bus, and I quickly spotted a public restroom sign right across the street from the bus stop. I pointed out the sign to David, and he nodded to indicate that I should go ahead and he would make sure he got my backpack off the roof of the bus. Never before had I appreciated the sight of a Chinese squat toilet more than at that very moment.

Walking back to the bus, I found David helping the bus driver get the luggage off the roof. It struck me that David had a servant's heart as he continued helping the driver even after he had located our bags. When all the bags had been unloaded, he gave the driver a handshake and a few friendly words of gratitude before patting me on the shoulder and telling me in Chinese, "Let's go." We walked down the main street for a few minutes, before taking a sharp left down a side street. It was not as crowded as I had expected and gotten used to from traveling throughout southern China, but I noticed David greeting just about everyone walking down the street as if they were old friends.

After walking for another twenty minutes, David opened the side gate of what seemed to be a fairly nice residence and motioned for me to go in first. In front of us was a beautiful garden with all kinds of flowers and a pathway leading up to a nice one-story house. David walked up to the house, opened the door and told his wife and in laws to come out and greet me. A moment later I was met by friendly smiles and warm hugs from this sweet family. The only one that was somewhat reserved and formal was the father-in-law who gave me a firm handshake and told me "Welcome to our city" in Mandarin Chinese with a slight smile on his face.

They took me inside, and we all sat down by the table to enjoy a warm bowl of the most delicious soup. David seemed to be the only one who spoke some English, and I tried my very best to communicate with the family with the limited Chinese I knew. Sometimes I had to ask David to translate for me, but thankfully they laughed along and had no problems with the fact that our communication was challenging.

David's daughter, only a few months old, was the cutest little baby with dark curly hair. His wife, Li Yue, was also very warm and welcoming, and although she spoke only a few words of English, she made sure I felt right at home and seemed very interested in hearing the story of what had brought me from Norway.

After a cup of tea and wonderful fellowship with the family, David told me he would take me to his sister-in-law's hotel up the road. I grabbed my backpack, and we drove about five minutes down the road to what seemed to be the only tall building in the entire city. David walked ahead of me to the reception desk and pulled his sister-in-law aside for a couple of minutes to make sure she was fully aware of what needed to be done to allow me to stay safely in the city for the next few days. Remember, a hotel receptionist would normally copy a guest's passport and fax it to the authorities to help them keep track of where foreigners are located at all times. However, thanks to this divine appointment, she didn't do that. She politely shook my hand, pulled a key from the key rack, and told me in a soft-spoken Chinese voice to follow her.

We climbed the stairs up to the third floor and walked down the hallway to my room. It was nothing fancy in itself and looked like an ordinary two-star hotel room, but the view was breathtaking. Green rolling hills stretched far into the distance, and white and yellow flowers covered the valley between the two ranges of snow-covered mountains leading

———

back out to Yining, where I had come from only this morning. Pulling the curtains to the side, I couldn't help but take a deep breath and exhale a quiet thank you to God for allowing me to walk through this extraordinary journey with Him. Once I got situated in my room, David asked me to join him for a walk around the town so he could show me around.

Have you ever thought about what it would be like to show up in a rural community where nobody has ever seen a foreigner before? Well, let me give you an idea. It felt much like everyone around me froze, as if time stood still, and David and I were the only ones moving. As we walked along the street, almost everyone who noticed us stopped what they were doing and just stood there staring, as if their minds could not comprehend that there was something different about me. I am positive to this day that it was not as extreme as it felt, but it took a while for me to get used to it. David took me down the street from the hotel and found what I assumed to be one of his favorite street restaurants. In small Chinese cities such as this one, it is quite common to find tiny restaurants where most of their business takes place on the side of the street. David walked up to the owner and ordered two portions of his favorite lo mien soup, a delicious local

———

pasta dish special to this part of China. A few moments later, the restaurant owner walked over to our knee-high street-side table and put the bowls in front of us. It smelled divine, but it was just about as spicy as I could tolerate without making a scene. I wish I could say that had never happened before, but I feel pretty confident about arguing that you have not tried real "spicy" food until you have been served authentic spicy Chinese food.

David and I spent the rest of the afternoon walking around beautiful Xinlien as he shared his heart-warming testimony with me in English. He had moved to Urumqi a few years back from his own hometown, a few hours from Xinlien. There he had met his young bride-to-be, Li Yue, and after a few months of courtship, they had returned to Xinlien to get married. After setting up their own little apartment in Urumqi to finish their college education, they had eventually run into my Norwegian-American friends, John and Sara, on the university campus. Little by little, the two men became good friends, and John was able to share the Gospel with David and Li Yue.

Like most other locals, David had never heard the true Gospel of Jesus before, apart from being told that Christianity was a "fairytale" Western religion. One day John laid a Chinese Bible in David's hands and gave him some guidance in how to best read it. Much like my friend Luke in Zhangjiajie, who had spent a full year reading through the Bible several times before presenting me with a notebook of questions, David spent the next several months studying his Bible and coming to John with questions. One day he fell on his knees in his living room and gave his life to Christ and immediately proclaimed to his wife that he had become a Christian. She had listened to David talking about Jesus for months at this point, so in just a few weeks, she also received salvation.

David and Li Yue were both radically changed and started praying together and seeking God's purpose for their lives. John discipled David, and Sara discipled Li Yue; before long, these new Christians were out on campus preaching the good news to their friends and contacts. David and Li Yue showed no fear of persecution as they felt the power of the Holy Spirit work through them when they surrendered to Him. By graduation, John and Li Yue had started several Bible groups around campus and led dozens of people to Christ through their fearless evangelism efforts. One day,

---

when David came home from running some errands for his wife, she shared the exciting news that they were expecting a baby. While overjoyed, they quickly came to realize that their tiny studio apartment on campus would not be suitable for raising a family. As they didn't have any other family living in Urumqi, they eventually agreed that it would be best for them to move to Xinlien to live close to Li Yue's family to give them the support they needed.

After the move, they lost contact with a lot of friends in Urumqi, including John and Sara, who had for some reason not heard about their plans to move to Xinlien. Despite moving to a new place where he didn't know anyone apart from his in-laws, David's drive to share the Gospel of Christ did not cease. In the following months, He started each day with prayer walks and sought God for guidance and wisdom regarding who to share the Gospel with. He was very aware of the fact that he had to be careful, as he was no longer in a large city where he wouldn't stand out for his Christian beliefs. If he made any sudden moves in this completely unreached city, he would quickly be persecuted for his faith in one way or another. Much like I had sought God's daily guidance for my journey over the last month from a situation

---

———

of despair in Sauda, Norway, to Xinlien, China, David had done the same to see God's mighty work unfold before him and through him in this unreached city and county.

Through diligently praying and seeking God for His agenda in the midst of a dark spiritual situation, he and his wife had seen about a dozen individuals from various parts of the city receive salvation. He had witnessed to hundreds more and had spent significant amounts of time building relationships with high officials in the city, but had not seen breakthrough there yet.

David told me his story with tears in his eyes; it was very apparent that his heart's desire was to see these lost people experience the truth and the true and living God and His love for them. He was a true pioneer, a missionary to his own people, and when he shared that his mother-in-law had come to faith only a few weeks before, he couldn't hold back his tears any longer. They were still praying and witnessing to Li Yue's father, and although his heart had significantly softened since they moved home, he was not at the place of surrender yet. David told me that God was without a doubt moving his father-in-law's heart through watching his wife experience the life and love only Jesus can bring to the depths of your heart.

———

David's story was marvelous, and each individual testimony was a beautiful story carefully crafted by the most powerful and indescribable architect there is, God, our heavenly Father Himself.

Chapter Twelve

WE HAD BEEN walking the streets of Xinlien for a couple of hours while David had done most of the talking. After sharing the testimony about his wife's parents he stopped, took a deep breath and sighed as he turned to me and shared his biggest struggle. He wasn't having much success in discipling the new believers he had led to Christ. Apart from his mother-in-law, he had gradually become discouraged over how difficult it was to regularly meet the new believers to build their faith and knowledge of the Word and see them mature in their walk with Christ. David's heart and desire, and what He had felt God had directed him to do, was plant a house fellowship church in Xinlien. He had no idea how to do this, as there was no way he could safely connect with all the believers apart from

———

meeting them face to face, one at a time. David could not risk persecution for himself, his family or the new believers and their families by engaging in any sort of electronic communication. It goes without saying that the Chinese government keeps a close watch on that since they regulate the Internet more than most nations in the world, not even allowing Facebook for their 1.3 billion people. David had tried to regularly meet with the new believers one on one, but had not cracked the code of how to gather them all in one place at the same time to start a church. Typically, days and even weeks would pass between each time he met with individual new believers, making it nearly impossible to set up any type of organized secret meeting.

I watched as David went from being enthusiastic and overjoyed as he shared all the miraculous things God had done in the midst of this unreached city to becoming visibly discouraged by the fact that he did not see how he could safely facilitate and start the first church in this region, ever. I felt God told me to spend a few minutes encouraging him. I told him that God works in mysterious ways, and I knew that He had not led me all the way here without a reason. I told him I believed God was about to do something outstanding

———

that would affect not only his life and mine, but also have ripple effects on the city of Xinlien and the region for decades to come. After I shared my full testimony about how God had led me there, he quickly regained his smile and laughed as he told me, "I am so excited that God has led you here, Tore. I cannot wait to see what He is going to do over the next few days!"

I met David at his house the next morning—he already had plans for the day. He always started his day with a prayer walk to spend time with God. As he had flooded Xinlien with prayers from every angle, he had begun to see people come to faith through the power of his testimony and the Word of God. Today we were going to drive a few minutes out of the city, back to the grassy hills that I had admired on our way into the city the day before. After our prayer walk, he wanted me to join him for a visit to a special family he had been witnessing to over the last few weeks. I made sure to ask David for guidelines about what I could and couldn't share, but he assured me that the family were very nice people and had no intention of reporting me to the government for staying in the region.

Before we made that visit, however, we stopped for our

prayer walk in a place that was nothing short of awe-inspiring. If you have ever seen the movie Heidi, the landscape looked somewhat like that as we climbed up the steep grassy hills surrounded by sheep, goats and the little children herding them. The snow-covered mountains far off in the distance on both sides of the valley reminded me of my home country, while also quickly making me realize that I was thousands of miles away from home. "I cannot believe I actually made it here!"

My experience of following God's direction and going from one divine appointment to another to get here was almost unreal, so much so that I could do nothing but look to the cloudless sky and praise Jesus for His overwhelming provision and goodness. He had walked before me and was with me in this moment, and He certainly would not leave me stranded now.

"God, let Your will be done in Xinlien as it is in heaven. Here I am, God. Please use me to spread Your good news and the Gospel of your Son, Jesus Christ!"

The mornings in Xinlien were pretty cold as the tall mountains covered the sun until mid morning. You could see

───────

the sunbeams hitting the spectacular mountains and slowly making their way down the mountainsides until they hit the tops of the grassy hills. It was ten o'clock or so when we reached the top of the hill that David had set his mind to summit. When we reached the top and stopped to catch our breath, we both marveled at the sight of the valley below us. A blanket of fog was slowly lifting from the valley, and we could clearly see Xinlien with its small population of about fifty thousand people down below us. Before I had a chance to speak, David started praying earnestly for an outbreak of God's power and deliverance in the city. He prayed in Chinese, so I could follow him only partially, but there was no doubt in my mind that his prayers came from the heart of a man who truly loved and cared about the people of Xinlien. We spent probably an hour praying and claiming the promises of God's Word to break down strongholds in the community below while sunbeams painted the valley with beautiful colors as the fog disappeared.

One thing that struck me about David was that he rarely ever talked about anything but Jesus and what He had done in and through his life. Walking beside this devoted disciple of Christ delivered a much-needed breath of fresh air into my

───────

spiritual life as I continued seeking God's will every single morning.

One huge challenge of being in Xinlien was the fact that I was unable to get in touch with my fiancée. She had now been traveling around Thailand with a mission team from Norway for about a month, and since I was here as an "undercover agent" of Christ, I could not risk my security or that of David and his family by engaging in any type of electronic communication with her. It had now been several days since I had last talked to my dear Stephanie or read one of her comforting e-mails. I simply had to resign myself to the fact that, for as long as I was to stay in Xinlien, I could only pray that she was safe and that God was watching over her, as He was me.

———

100

Chapter Thirteen

LATER THE SAME day we walked up to a beautiful mansion located on the outskirts of the city. It belonged to a wealthy Mongol family, but David had given me very little information about the man. We were greeted at the door with very polite handshakes and quickly guided inside by inviting hand gestures to sit down around their dining room table. Almost everywhere in this part of China, tables sat about a foot off the ground; it was common to sit on pillows around the table. At mealtime, everyone receives a bowl of rice and chopsticks and then helps themselves to delicious meats and vegetable dishes placed in the middle of the table using the chopsticks. The gentleman sat down at the head of the table, and he wore a beautiful golden outfit unlike anything I had seen before. He had an unusual maroon-colored hat on his head and a silk scarf around his neck, also gold colored. The gentleman invited us to please help ourselves to the food and the warm tea his wife was in the process of serving. We had a wonderful conversation with the help of some translation by David, but our host was very inspired by the fact that I had traveled all the way from Norway at my young age. He was awestruck by my testimony and simple faith in God as we shared the Gospel with him.

At the end of the visit, he gave me a long handshake with both hands before he ceremonially lifted the golden scarf off his neck and put it around mine. I had no idea of the significance of this custom at the time and politely thanked him the best way I knew how. He then brought a maroon-colored hat just like the one he was wearing and proudly placed it on my head. After a few more minutes, David and I left. I never saw the man again, but I have kept his gifts for all of these years together with numerous other gifts I received during my many mission trips. As I was writing this book, I thought I would research the significance of these gifts, as I had never taken the time to do so. The scarf, also referred to as a khadag, is one of the most honorable gifts a Mongol can give out of respect to his guests. The colors have specific meanings regarding the recipient. The golden scarf I was given symbolizes knowledge and religion and is typically offered to educational or religious teachers. I am assuming that because we shared the Gospel with him, he found it appropriate to honor us as religious teachers. The hat has a different meaning. A hat is considered a very private and personal item to Mongols and is rarely used as a gift. Giving the gift of a hat could symbolize that the giver is in debt to the recipient.

The exciting thing about walking in obedience to God's day-to-day direction and His divine appointments is that you don't see what God has done to prepare the way, and you rarely see what God does in the life of the individual after your paths cross. You are simply allowing yourself to be a piece of a larger masterpiece of God's incredible and caring work for each lost soul that He is trying to call home to His heart. Oftentimes I wonder what position this gentleman held in the town of Xinlien and whether there were ripple effects from the seeds of God's Word planted in his heart that day. Only God knows for sure as He sees the past, present and future all at the same time. We don't need to know it all; we just need to know that every hour of the day matters, and He has divine appointments that are ready for us to step into. These are not based on our qualifications or reputation, but on the fact that we love Jesus and that we love our neighbor as ourselves. Out of that love, you can be a missionary wherever you are, whenever God directs. Listen to His heart. Ask Him to use you just as you are to make a difference, and prepare yourself to be amazed at how He leads your steps into situations where you are able to minister to hearts that are desperate to hear and see God's love demonstrated.

If you allow this book to speak to your heart about only one thing, that would be my desire-know that God is not looking for a perfect individual to minister to the lost; He is looking for a willing heart. Whether that heart belongs to a newly saved seventeen year old who knows little about the world around him or a lady in her nineties at the end of her life journey who has seen the world change more than most can grasp, it makes no difference. It starts with a humble prayer such as this one:

"God, I realize it is by Your amazing grace that I am saved, and I am forever grateful for Your love and care for me. You have finished the work for me, and You want me to live my life to the fullest and experience heaven on earth.

———

Here I am, God; use me. Allow me to be a tool in Your hands to speak and show Your love and truth to someone in need today. Show me what to do, what to say, and send people my way who need someone to demonstrate Your love and care for them today."

Whatever situation you are in, it all boils down to this simple phrase: "Here I am, God; use me." Every time I opened my black Norwegian Bible, I looked at the sentence I had written on the inside of the cover page: "Are you still willing to go to the ends of the earth for Me?" You only have to be willing—He will do the rest.

———

Chapter Fourteen

T HE NEXT DAY we had plans to go for a hike about an hour outside of Xinlien, deeper into the valley, to visit another of David's contacts. Before we left town, we went to a local gift shop and picked up a five-pound bag of salt and a large box of local tea called Suutei Tsai, a Mongolian type of tea usually mixed with milk and salt before it is served. David explained to me that it was customary to bring a gift when visiting families like the one we were going to today. We loaded the gifts in a backpack and started our drive into the valley. The tall snow-covered mountains that isolated Xinlien from the world around it were getting closer and closer together, and I saw them merge in the distance, the landscape gradually turning into rolling hills. We drove a long while on a muddy country road that twisted and turned up the steep inclines of the grass-covered hills. Eventually David parked the car and told me we had to walk the rest of the distance. We quickly took a path that led off the muddy road and took us over a hilltop, down a slope and then up another steep hill. While walking in ankle-deep grass, we watched a herd of sheep all around us having the time of their lives feasting on a plenteous supply of fresh, green grass. After a couple more steep climbs, we arrived at a rather large farm consisting of several buildings. It was nothing like the dark red three-story barns I was used to seeing in Norway. All the flat-roofed buildings were painted white. A few chickens and sheep milled about in the fenceless courtyard as we approached the entrance of the main building. This remote farm with its breathtaking views over the grassy hills exuded an atmosphere of peace. As I attempted to take it all in, an elderly man came out and welcomed us with a big hug. I quickly offered him the Suutei Tsai tea and the bag of salt out of my backpack, and he expressed his deep appreciation as he handed it over to his wife who came walking up to us from the house about then. After greeting and thanking us, she ran back into the kitchen and began carrying plates and side dishes into a building next to the main building.

———

After a few minutes of conversation in the courtyard, the man invited us to come inside and make ourselves comfortable as he said with a laugh, "I hope you built up an appetite climbing those hills!" That was the case, but I always wondered what I would be served in a new place. I was pretty confident it would be nothing out of the ordinary, like the snake soup or dog stew I'd had the pleasure of eating a few years before in south China while traveling with an evangelism team. Whatever it was smelled somewhat familiar as the women continued carrying dishes past us and putting them down on the floor in the center of the building we were entering.

"Wow!" I exclaimed in surprise as I stepped over the threshold. The room was like nothing I had ever seen before! The wide-open, large room had almost nothing on the colorful carpeted floor, but along all four walls were tall stacks of what appeared to be hundreds of neatly folded blankets in the most amazing combinations of bright colors. Along with the blankets were enough mattresses and pillows to comfortably give a whole village a good night's sleep. I could only conclude that this was their multipurpose family bedroom, family room and dining room as the food was

———

being served in the middle of the blanketed floor. Before long a young lady came in and started pulling down pillows from the tall stacks and arranging them in a nice big circle around the food on the floor. "Please, please, make yourself at home!" the man urged as he sat down on one of the pillows on the floor and made hand gestures for us to do the same.

As we sat down, the young lady started pouring us warm Suutei Tsai tea, and I tried my very best to keep my facial expressions under control as I slowly sipped on it. The flavored salt-water taste quickly numbed my tongue to a place where I could tolerate it, but it was not at all pleasant tasting initially. My tastebuds quickly came back to life as the wife carried in the main dish, a large leg of lamb, served on a huge silver platter beautifully decorated with all kinds of steamed vegetables. Little did they know that Norwegians eat lamb year round, from smoked lamb ribs on Christmas Eve, to leg of lamb for Easter and a special lamb and cabbage stew during the fall. Few meals would make my mouth water like a good leg of lamb, so that made my day right there.

We spent what seemed like hours talking and laughing while eating the delicious food. Like any other visit we had made so far, David was quick to help translate for me whenever I got stuck mid sentence due to my limited Chinese vocabulary. Our hosts were very interested as I shared my story of getting to Xinlien and how Jesus had touched and changed my life and brought me into more adventure than I could ever dare to dream of. The evening ended with us praying together before we went back outside and made our way back down to the car as the sun was setting behind the snow-covered mountains. We barely made it back to the car before it turned pitch black dark.

Driving down the mountainside in the dark was quite an experience in itself, but it was unmatched by the moving visit we'd had with the Mongolian family up on their mountain farm. Little did I know at the time who they were, what role they played in what God was doing in the region or how our visit had impacted that family's direction and the lives of everyone they had influence over going forward. I fell asleep that night in my hotel room surrounded by the sweet peace of knowing that God was doing something miraculous in our midst.

Chapter Fifteen

THE NEXT MORNING started like most other mornings so far while visiting Xinlien, with a prayer walk around town together with David. Never before had I met such a prayer warrior. The closest I could compare him to would be my mother who had always been my role model when it came to prayer. Growing up I had witnessed how she would spend a good two hours every morning in her bedroom, praying, interceding, reading the Word and worshipping like only a mother can worship while keeping time with her Ron Kenoly or Lindell Cooley worship CDs using her feet on the wooden floor.

David impressed me, and his passion to intercede spoke deep into my heart about the love that he had for the lost souls of all the people in the valley. The majority of them had never heard the Gospel, and due to the fact that he could not openly share the Gospel, there were few other ways to spread God's love other than to witness and share the good news one relationship and friendship at a time. At the same time, heavy spiritual strongholds rested over the area—effects from shamanism, ancestral worship and other religious activity exercised by a lot of the older generations in the area. Slowly but surely, David's prayers had been answered and cleared the way for divine appointments, where he had been able to speak straight into the hearts of influential people in the county. One by one, people had received salvation, been given God's Word and started their walk with Christ.

The one thing that was missing and that would make a major impact in the city moving forward was a fellowship of Christians where they could meet, pray, support and disciple each other and together move forward with much greater power and impact. I didn't know for sure what God had in store, but I had a feeling all along that He was going to do something remarkable before I left the area.

That very day was going to be something out of the ordinary, if I could call any day out of the ordinary on my journey over the last few weeks. The entire journey had been

———

anything but ordinary, but this day was going to prove to be the highlight, the climax, the summit of the mission on which God had sent me.

During our prayer walk that morning, David and I prayed earnestly for a church to be planted in Xinlien; we prayed with expectation and determination for God to act in a way only He could. Where it was humanly impossible for David to reach out to all of the people he had led to Christ in a safe manner and get them to all gather in the same location at the same time, we quickly got a feeling that God was up to something miraculous as one Christ follower after another crossed paths with us that morning. Through our prayer walk, David had felt that God told him to set a time and place for a gathering, not knowing how many people would show, if any at all.

The first young man we ran into while walking down the streets was one of the first people David had led to Christ after coming to Xinlien. He was an on-fire believer, and his eyes lit up as David asked him if we could use his apartment for a gathering at six thirty that evening. His apartment was on the second floor of a building not too far from where we were standing, and it was right in the heart of downtown Xinlien.

———

We did not tell him about the scope of what we were believing God for; we simply told him to expect David and me to show up there later to pray together and share the Gospel.

Only a few minutes later, we heard another young man calling for David who spotted us from across the street. He zigzagged across the street among the moving traffic and gave David a big hug and introduced himself to me politely. It wasn't difficult to see that God's love was shining out of his heart and that he was carrying a light in the darkness that he wanted other people to experience. We told him about our meeting that night, and he said he would definitely be there.

One person after another, I kid you not, approached us as we kept praying and walking up and down the streets. Divine appointments! God was placing them in our path! By lunchtime, we had invited eleven people to our meeting that night, and everyone had accepted the invitation. As we found a noodle kitchen and sat down for lunch, David told me with tears in his eyes, "Tore, that was all the people I have led to Christ over the last few months. This is incredible! I have only met each of them a couple of times since I can't contact them safely in any way other than meeting them in person.

———

Apart from my mother-in-law, that was all of them. I cannot believe we actually managed to arrange a meeting for all of them to gather together!"

———

Chapter Sixteen

THE AFTERNOON FLEW by, and we walked to David's friend's apartment around six o'clock to prepare for the meeting. To avoid raising suspicions, we approached the building casually and made our way up to the apartment to knock quietly on the door. Our host let us in, but the lights were off, and he told us to make sure we stayed far away from the windows that had no curtains or blinds to avoid being visible to people on the street. He led us to a back bedroom where he had pushed the bed up against the wall to make room for us to sit on the floor. He had no idea yet that we were still expecting ten more people to come, and when we told him, his eyes went as wide as a deer caught in the headlights. David calmed him down and assured him, "God is in control. He has arranged this and will protect us

———

from any danger."

Before long, we heard one quiet knock after another on the front door in the dim hallway. It was dark outside, but the street lamps were shining into the windows of the apartment and lit up the ceilings. A few minutes after six thirty, we were all there—eleven local new believers; David, who had known Christ only a couple of years; and me, a young missionary from Norway. Everyone sat on the floor in the dark bedroom with their eyes wide open, hungry to hear God's Word.

David opened the meeting by sharing his heart and explaining the purpose of our gathering. He reassured everyone of their safety, while letting them know that we were being cautious for a very good reason. David started crying as he poured out his heart and love for his disciples and shared his gratitude over the fact that God had brought them all together. He prayed for the group and then introduced me.

I shared my heart and delivered an unprepared message about how crucial it was for believers to regularly meet and pray for each other, and to support and care for each other as a group. God was speaking through me; I felt I had little control over what was coming out of my mouth. God was

———

using my testimony and story to lay the foundation of the beginning of the first church of Xinlien.

When I finished, David took over again and poured out his desire to meet with the group weekly moving forward, and they all agreed on a time that worked for everyone. The enthusiasm in the group was evident despite the fact that everyone was still whispering to each other in the dark. We spent the last half hour of the meeting praying for the individual needs of these new believers before leaving the apartment one by one to head down the dark stairway and back to our homes.

The foundation had been laid, and the church had been planted! David was dancing down the back alleys leading back to the hotel as he rejoiced in the Lord over His mighty work. Everyone had committed to the vision and mission of the new church, and they had set a permanent meeting time that would enable the group to gather once a week moving forward.

That night as I laid my head on the pillow, I felt God spoke to Me and said, "Well done, Tore. You have completed your task here, and I need you to start your journey back to Urumqi tomorrow. I will lead you on from there." My eyes welled up with tears as I thought about the unbelievable journey God had allowed me to experience thus far, and I was overjoyed about the miraculous answer to prayer that had taken place that very night. At the same time, my heart was breaking that I was about to leave David and probably would never see him or his family again here in this life. However, I also felt an immense peace as I laid in the hotel bed, a feeling of being in the middle of God's will and seeing Him move in a mighty way despite my lack of qualifications, experience, money or prestige. How could I ever want to live my life in any other way?

As I peered out the hotel window the next morning, it seemed as if there was a whole different spiritual atmosphere resting over the city—a feeling of breakthrough, hope and light. I did not sense the oppression and heaviness that we had battled every morning during our prayer walks. God was certainly doing a work in our midst, far greater than I could have ever dared to dream of or imagine. I was so grateful for the opportunity to play a small part in it, a part of being in the right place at the right time, in God's timing.

I said my goodbyes to David and his sweet family, and he

followed me back to the bus stop where I had so comically sprinted to the restroom after getting off the bus about a week and a half before. The pain I felt now was much different—it was the pain of saying goodbye to good friends I'd likely never see again.

I boarded the bus together with a large crowd of locals and a couple of chickens, and off we went. The trip that had seemed to last forever going into Xinlien seemed to be over before it ever started on the way out. The beautiful mountains were further and further apart as we left the valley, until I could barely see them in the distance. The vivid green hills gradually turned into flat fields of grass and rice and, soon enough, the city of Yining appeared before my eyes. It was about two o'clock in the afternoon when I got off of the bus, so I figured I would explore the city a little bit before finding myself a motel for the night. David had arranged for me to ride with a friend of his that was headed from this town back to Urumqi the next morning. Since I had flown to Yining on the way to Xinlien, I had no idea what was in store for me, but that was the last thing on my mind at the moment.

Chapter Seventeen

I HURRIED TO find an Internet cafe where I could check my e-mail to see if I had any updates from Stephanie. I had been without Internet for nearly two weeks, so my heart was pounding as I eventually found a small place on a street corner. After listening to the now-archaic dial-up Internet tone, I logged into my account and saw several e-mails from Stephanie, but none from the last week. But an e-mail from her grandmother did catch my eye. As I began reading, in a split second my heart sank to the ground. I could barely breathe as I read the message telling me that my bride-to-be had been in a horrific car accident! While her grandmother didn't have many details, she said Stephanie was currently hospitalized, but that she was going to be okay. She related that the team car had driven off the side of the road and flipped several times on the way down a steep, muddy mountain slope. Miraculously, none of the team members had been seriously injured. She promised to keep me posted as she had more information.

The e-mail was from the day before, so I figured the accident must have happened just a day or two before that. My face was white as could be as I tried to catch my breath after the initial shock, and I felt I might throw up. All I wanted to do was hold my precious Stephanie in my arms and care for her, or even just comfort her. I couldn't shake off the shock, so I ended up closing my computer and dropping my head to the table. As tears streamed down my face, I felt further away from Stephanie than I ever had before. It was bad enough that I had not talked to her for two weeks, but now I couldn't even be there for her when she needed me most. Even the two years we'd spent on opposite sides of the planet after my first trip to China felt minor in comparison to this moment. She was only a few hours south of me by plane, but I had no way of getting to her. My bank account was nearly empty, and I had no way of calling her or any information about what hospital she was at.

A couple of minutes passed during which I felt as alone

and heartbroken as I had ever felt in my life. Then, an incredible peace started flowing through my body. It felt as though a soft, warm blanket had been placed over my shoulders and someone was hugging me while helping me back into an upright position. God knew exactly what I needed in that moment, and He started speaking to me in His still, small voice, comforting me and ensuring me that He had this. He told me that Stephanie was going to be fine and that His angels were watching over her, as they had been watching over me.

I dried the tears off my face, lifted my head and started reading the many e-mails my darling had sent to me several days before the accident. I smiled as she related counting down the days to our wedding day, something we had been doing for a very long time. We were both greatly anticipating being able to start our journey together as a married couple. It had been about three years since we first met in Jamaica, and my love for her was deeper and stronger than ever before. I had never been more certain about anything in my life than the fact that we were going to share the rest of our lives together.

As I continued to read, it was clear that Stephanie had

been having a wonderful time in Thailand prior to the accident. My heart gradually warmed up and the color slowly returned to my face as I read one e-mail after another. She was so sweet and funny, and I was truly so blessed to have her love me and choose me as her future husband.

After reading the last email, I wrote back to both Stephanie and Mema, her grandmother, to let them know that I had received the news, and that I was praying for God to move in the situation. I was aching to hear Stephanie's voice, but I knew there was no way to reach her at the moment, so I'd just have to hope that could happen sooner rather than later.

As I left the shop, I found myself walking aimlessly down the street. It was still the middle of the day, and I was still under God's complete guidance, protection and provision. I pondered whether God perhaps still had great things in store for the rest of the trip or whether I had completed my mission and the rest of the trip was just returning to Hong Kong. While I had no idea, I did know that I felt emotionally drained from learning about Stephanie's accident.

As I continued down the street, I saw a small jewelry store

———

and decided to see if I could find a special gift for Stephanie, a gift in memory of the moment we were in—both completely dependent on God on separate missions, but both safely in the hands of God and protected by His angels.

I found a pair of beautiful little heart-shaped earrings with a small diamond in the center. It was probably not a diamond, but as I didn't know any Chinese names for gemstones, it wouldn't have helped me much to ask. They were pretty, and I knew Stephanie would love them. What was really neat was that the pair I had pointed out was only a display item and the skilled goldsmith started making the earrings right before my eyes by melting a small piece of gold. In about twenty minutes, I held a pair of earrings that looked identical to the ones I had chosen from his display counter.

Choosing that small gift for Stephanie and anticipating giving it to her when I saw her again in a few weeks helped me focus more on everything that lay ahead of us and less on the pain of the present. God even spoke to me in that moment about how He can take our brokenness and make something very beautiful and precious out of it.

———

Chapter Eighteen

THE NEXT MORNING I walked up to the terminal where David had told me to meet his friend, and sure enough, he sat waiting for me in his white jeep. Another passenger was already in the front passenger seat, so I had the back seat to myself. For the next twelve hours or so, we witnessed the most breathtaking mountainous landscape I had ever seen—but we also drove on the worst roads I had been on since my trip to the Blue Mountains in Jamaica three years earlier. The memories of sitting shoulder to shoulder with my sweetheart while driving up the muddy road to the tallest mountain in Jamaica came streaming back to me as the Jeep was put to one test after another while navigating the steep roads.

We made a few stops along the way, but for the most part

we were in the middle of nowhere surrounded by such beauty that I quite honestly struggle to describe it with words. As we pulled up to the Urumqi university where my old friends John and Sara had showed me such wonderful hospitality a few weeks earlier, I was bursting with excitement to tell them about the adventure God had allowed me to be part of. I was hoping they were home because, at that point, I had no other place to go, nor did I have any other plans or directions from God about where to go next.

God reminded me of His faithful guidance as I walked up the stairway to their apartment. This was the exact same place where God had told me to stop, without any clue that this apartment building, out of the dozens of others looking just like it, would be the one where John and Sara lived. What an awesome God I serve, so personal and interested in the smallest details of my life. His love for me consumed me in an instant and reenergized me as I knocked on their door.

Sara, obviously happy to see me, spoke in Norwegian as she invited me in and asked me to tell them everything! The next couple of days I did nothing but fellowship, eat, sleep and get rested up. God didn't give me any further direction, but I did feel I needed to just be a blessing to the family that had so generously opened up their home to me. I cooked, cleaned and helped them with their kids.

Finally, a couple of days later, I was able to reach Stephanie by phone! She had e-mailed that she was out of the hospital and couldn't wait to hear from me, and I didn't waste a second. I immediately called the number she'd given me. Although we couldn't talk very long as it cost a fortune to call Thailand, the minutes seemed liked hours. She described the accident, relating how they had been traveling up a narrow mountain road to their next outreach location in a large pickup truck, with all of the girls in the backseat, the team leader in the front seat and two guys on the truck bed. Nobody had been wearing seat belts, but that wasn't uncommon in that part of the world. The driver suddenly swerved to miss some kind of animal, which led to the truck veering off the road and flipping down a hillside, leveling vegetation on the way. The guys in the truck bed were ejected first and saw the vehicle fly over their heads as it kept rolling down the mountain with the rest of the team and the driver inside. Stephanie said it seemed like the truck rolled seven or eight times before it came to a hard stop about half way down the slope. There, "randomly" placed on the slanted slope, was a large old tree trunk that had fallen over, sturdy enough to stop the truck from continuing its path all the way to the bottom of the hill.

The truck landed on its roof, with broken glass everywhere, but everyone was able to crawl out alive with no major injuries! Though overjoyed by the fact that they were alive and that God had miraculously saved their lives using a tree, they were still terrified from the shock of having been in such great danger.

Stephanie had bruises and cuts from glass, but said she felt fine after crawling out of the wreckage. She immediately noticed that two male team members were nowhere to be found. Afraid she would find them dead somewhere between the wreck and the top of the hill, she started yelling their names and crawling back up the muddy slope by grabbing onto roots and whatever was left of bushes and trees. She didn't see them anywhere, and every minute that passed increased her fear that she and the others would find them dead. After making it past pieces of luggage and debris from the truck, they found one of the men lying close to the top of the hill, bleeding from his head and in shock, but otherwise fine.

As the team tended to their injured teammate, the other missing team member came running down the road followed by several cars that he had called on to help. He had somehow jumped off the truck bed just before it went over the edge and taken off running for help as he saw the truck flipping down the mountainside. The guy lying at the top of the hill said he had been thrown off during the first flip and had seen the truck fly right over his head as he hit the ground on his back.

The most serious injury among all the team members was suffered by one of the girls, who broke her collarbone. Besides that, they had only bruises, cuts and scratches from all the broken glass. It was truly a miracle. The Thailand team had already planned to pull back to a retreat for the last bit of their two-month stay, so they just made an early start on that part of their trip after what happened.

Of course, I was relieved to know that Stephanie was okay and that her team would be able to relax and enjoy the rest of their stay despite their injuries; but I also found myself dwelling on the fact that I was and am to this day dependent on God to protect the ones I love. As much as I want to be there and make sure my family is safe, I cannot be there every hour of the day. I need to prayerfully trust God to keep His hand of protection over them as they head off to school and work. I must trust that He is present around them with His angels at all times.

Chapter Nineteen

BEIJING! ONE MORNING during my quiet time while still in Urumqi, I felt that God was telling me to get on a train to Beijing. I knew a contact who should be in Beijing, and I reached out by e-mail in hopes that he would be able to host me there for a few days. The contact was my ninth-grade English teacher, Robert, who was serving there as a "tentmaker" together with his wife and kids. Though I hadn't been in touch with him since he moved there, amazingly enough, he responded that same day to say I was more than welcome to stay at their home and even celebrate Norway's National Day with them on May 17.

A few days later, I boarded an old run-down train for the 2000-mile trip from Urumqi to Beijing. I had been on a few long train rides during my short life, but none that compared to the length of this one. John said I could expect to arrive in Beijing in about fifty-two hours!

The train car I entered had two sets of three-bed bunks, and I put my stuff on the top bunk so I could hopefully get some rest along the way. The mattresses were about an inch thick and extremely uncomfortable, but it would have to do for the next two nights. Between the three bunks was a narrow table, and the bottom bunks were used for seating.

I lost count of the number of fascinating locals I met during the journey, but a few farmers stayed with me for a good bit of it. They had brought along some undercooked horsemeat and ridiculously strong liquor, and as the Chinese like to do, they invited me to eat and drink along with them. I politely took a small bite of the meat, but explained that I didn't drink alcohol and they fortunately had no problem with that. Those fifty-two hours seemed to last for a week, but the many interesting conversations and jolly laughter from the semi-drunk, horsemeat-eating farmers surely helped the time pass more quickly.

Beijing! The smog-covered megacity with apartment buildings touching the sky as far as the eye could see was visible out the train windows. Once we arrived and I got off the train, I found myself unsteady on my feet. It took a few minutes to get my land legs back after spending all that time on a moving train. The sight of locals walking around with masks on their face due to the pollution was something for which I had not mentally prepared myself. I certainly hadn't thought to purchase one for myself, and I really couldn't see myself wearing one anyway.

I pulled out the address where my English teacher and his family were living and hopefully expecting my arrival. If you have never been in a megacity with a population of fifteen million, it would probably be hard to imagine the overwhelming number of people, cars, bicycles and apartment buildings. The taxi ride was simply breathtaking in the sense that I had never before been in such a massive city with a never-ending scene of crowded streets. On the way, we passed by awe-inspiring sights such as the Forbidden City and the Temple of Heaven. A good hour later, the taxi pulled up in front of a large apartment complex, probably twenty stories high. After paying the driver, I showed the guard in front of the building the name of my old english teacher. A few minutes later Robert´s daughter came down to greet me and to lead me up to their apartment.

The sweet and hospitable Norwegian family lived in a large apartment on the fifteenth floor with a beautiful view out over the city. I quickly settled in as they offered me a nice home-cooked Norwegian dinner, and we spent the next couple of hours getting caught up. They were very curious to hear what I was doing traveling around China on my own with nothing but a backpack and what I had experienced so far, and I wanted to find out how they were experiencing life in ministry in China as I could very well see myself in a similar situation later on in life.

The next few days was more of a retreat to me than the adventure of walking in uncertainty that I had experienced over the previous weeks of traveling through China on my own. The family, and particularly their daughter and her friends who were all my age, did their best to show me what Beijing had to offer. I remember one night we went to a trendy coffee and karaoke bar close by to meet some of their friends, and to my surprise, one of them was an old friend and roommate from my days in Hong Kong. I couldn't believe that I had run into an old friend in a city of fifteen million people in the middle of China. After the emotional roller coaster of Stephanie's horrific car accident in Thailand, God knew exactly what I needed to encourage me. David and I hung out for a couple of days, and he showed me what his life as a Chinese student in Beijing was like; he was there to study the language for a year or two. I have no doubt that running into him that evening was a divine appointment orchestrated by God not only to encourage me, but also to encourage David since he had been discouraged and starting to doubt whether he was really supposed to be there. My story and our friendship helped him. When we said goodbye a few days later, he was once again fired up about taking the Gospel to the world.

One of the absolute highlights of my time in Beijing was a trip to the Great Wall of China. It wasn't just an ordinary visit to one of the touristy parts of the wall that has been rebuilt to handle the massive number of visitors, but a visit to the authentic Great Wall. I traveled with a group of four others a couple of hours outside of Beijing and parked our car close to the Wall. We saw only a few farms and houses around us as we hiked up a trail to the ancient ruins of the wall. After walking about an hour, we came to a part of the wall and a few towers that were more or less intact to the point that we

_____

could safely walk into them and walk on the wall from one tower to the next. Eventually, we found a tower that had plenty of room to set up a camp, make a fire and pull out our sleeping bags to spend the night. The feeling of lying down to sleep on top of a two-thousand-year-old man-made structure that can be seen from space was epic. As I gazed up at the millions of stars in the night sky, I thanked God from the bottom of my heart for His amazing love and care for me. This was just what I needed after all I had been through—to be surrounded by friends, doing something crazy fun and creating a memory for life. It was certainly an unforgettable experience.

The following morning, we hiked back down to our car and went back to the big city. My host family and I celebrated Norwegian National Day on May 17, just a few days later. The entire family dressed up in their nicest clothes and let me borrow some as well, since I certainly had not brought Sunday clothes along in my backpack. We went to the Norwegian Embassy in Beijing and celebrated the day together with about two hundred other Norwegians who lived in Beijing. This experience meant that I had now celebrated our Norwegian National Day on four different continents

_____

over the last five years. This time around, we had enough people to walk in the traditional Norwegian parade, waiving our Norwegian flags and shouting, "Hip-hip-hurray!" This is a cheer of celebration and freedom for our people. The feeling of unity and patriotism in the midst of a foreign country surrounded by people I did not know, yet who had the same Viking blood running through their veins, was memorable to say the least. It gave me a boost of strength to continue my journey.

A few days later I said goodbye to my former teacher and his family who had been so kind to open their home to me and departed Beijing. I had started counting down the days until my return trip to Norway, which was now less than two weeks out. After my stay in Beijing, I felt peace with God that my mission in China was completed and went ahead and purchased a one-way ticket back to Norway. I traveled by plane back to Hong Kong and was able to spend the last week with my friends and base leaders there.

I lost count of how many times I shared my testimony regarding this trip I was on, but what I noticed was that every time I shared the story, I was able to connect more dots of how God had prepared the way and created a masterpiece in

———

which He simply wanted me to participate. He could have chosen anyone with a willing heart, but He chose me. Had I not been willing to get out of my bed that morning about two months earlier in faith that God would heal me from my back injury, I would have missed the incredible adventure God was offering to allow me to experience. Had I not listened for His voice in the first place through prayerfully seeking Him through reading His Word, I would not have heard His still, small voice telling me to quit my job and buy a one-way ticket to China. Had I believed in the circumstances more than I did in God's miracle-working power, I would have had plenty of excuses to stay put and miss out big time.

———

Chapter Twenty

WHAT IS GOD telling you through this story, my friend? What is He speaking to you about doing as far as walking in His will for your life? From my personal experience, I can tell you that walking the line of grace and obedience to the Creator of the universe is no simple task, and certainly not something at which you will succeed every day of your life. At times, you will feel close to God, but moments will also come when you feel far away. The truth is, He dwells in your heart by His Holy Spirit and is closer than you can imagine.

If you go through a time when you turn away and distance yourself from God—and only you know the reason why—all you have to do is turn around; He will be right there! What I am trying to say is, there will never be a time when you feel

———

fully qualified and prepared to be used for His glory and to be a missionary to the world around you. Thankfully, He is looking for your willing heart, not your capabilities, He has work for you to do, but most of all He wants to show you that He loves you and that He wants you to live your life to the fullest.

Every single day, you pass by dozens and maybe even hundreds of people, all with different stories. Some of those stories are joyful, thanks to God's love working in and through them; but all too often, the stories are heartbreaking and dark. These people need someone to step into their path, to be a "divine appointment" on their journey, to help them direct their focus towards the true source of joy and life, Jesus. What can you do today to make a difference in the lives of others? How can you shine God's marvelous light and life into your surroundings and your everyday life?

The challenge has been extended, and for you to accept it and experience the matchless miracles God has in store specifically for you, you will need to do just one thing: step out of your comfort zone!

Your comfort zone is what keeps you away from anything

———

new, and it is in fact what keeps you away from growth and from making a difference. To step out into the unknown, you need to be brave and trust that God will give you the strength you need in the moment you need it, that He will provide you with the words to speak as you open your mouth to share His love and Gospel. You need to trust that God will provide the finances if He tells you to do something that you are not able to provide for in your own power. I wrote this short book in the hope that it will help you in those moments when God speaks to you with His still, small voice. When He tells you to do something—whether seemingly small and insignificant or along the lines of quitting your job and buying a one-way ticket to a foreign country—trust that if God was there for me, He will be there for you. He is yesterday, today and forever the same God, the same Father and the same Provider, for you and for me and for everyone else with whom you share your life. He has a personalized plan for all of His children, and He wants you to experience heaven on earth and live your life to the fullest.

If your Bible is like mine, it contains literally thousands of promises that God has extended to us, for us to know and declare throughout our day to combat the enemy and his constant attacks. The Creator of the Universe is for us, so who can be against us? Jesus told His disciples in John 15:16 that, "You did not choose Me but I chose you, and appointed you that you would go and bear fruit, and that your fruit would remain, so that whatever you ask of the Father in My name He may give to you."

You may think that God told that to His disciples and not to you. They were, after all, around Jesus 24/7 and were "qualified" to bear fruit and be His witnesses to the ends of the earth. But who were these disciples? They included several fishermen, a tax collector, a politician and a thief who had never heard about Jesus before they met Him one day and dropped everything they had to follow Him. He told them, "Lay down your own and follow Me." He did not tell them to spend four years in a Bible college and get a fancy degree and then maybe He would find them worthy to be used for His glory. Don't get me wrong—there is nothing wrong with devoting four years of your life to study the Word of God; but it does not need to be a prerequisite to serve God in your day-to-day life. God did not ask His disciples to go to seminary, or to read or memorize the Scriptures, or to make sure they were free of sinful behavior, or to make sure their

———

heart was in the right place. He simply said, "Follow me, and I will show you how."

He is still saying these words to you today, wherever you are. He is still saying those words to me as I am writing this book—which He, by the way, told me to write so that you could read this story and allow God to speak to your heart through it.

Jesus is saying, "Follow me, and I will show you how." He is here in our midst by His Holy Spirit. All you need to do is calm your heart, turn off your cell phone and any other distraction you may have allowed to be part of your daily routine and listen. It may come to you right away, or it may take days or weeks. If you listen, He will speak. If you walk through the grocery store and pray to God to show you someone who needs encouragement, He will surely not take long to tug your heart as someone walks by you.

If you are willing to lay down a moment of your day, your entire day, your entire week or your entire life, He will surely not fail to give you direction. He is forever faithful, and He is forever loving and gracious. He does not see your failures or your shortcomings, since they were forgiven through His

———

work on the cross; He only aches for you to come "home" to His embrace, to allow yourself to be His son or daughter and experience the love that only He can show you. He wants you to love your neighbor as yourself and be a light to the world, and all He is looking for is for your heart to be willing.

Epilogue

T HE BALL IS now in your court; be inspired to step out of your own comfort zone to experience all of the incredible things He has in store for you—today. Turn to Him and say, "Here I am, Lord; use me." When you fail and fall back into your selfish ways and close God out of your life, tell Him, "Here I am, Lord; use me." When everything feels dry and you see no hope in the midst of a difficult situation, tell Him, "Here I am, Lord. I need You to step in and show me Your love." Your answer will most likely come from a willing son or daughter of God that moments earlier prayed to the same God asking to be used for His glory. Can you see how this works?

Does God need you to participate in building His Kingdom and sharing His love and truth on earth? Yes, absolutely yes! Look at the world around you. Can you make a difference alone? Yes, and no. God needs His people to stand up together, get out of their comfortable bleachers and into the world and be the light that God called them to be in the midst of darkness. He is calling us to not only make a difference but also to be the difference in the world. Do you remember the song, "This Little Light of Mine"? Sing that to yourself as you get out there in the dark world. Where there is light, the darkness must flee. Darkness is, in fact, the absence of light.

Paul told the church in Ephesus, "But now you are light in the Lord. Walk as children of light." Did you notice that he used the word "walk" and not "sit"? You are to walk into the dark places of the world and be a light. How? Just do it, and your faithful God will show you how to make a difference. Just go, and He will surely step in at the perfect time and do a miraculous work through you. I don't mean to advertise for any specific company here, but "Just do it!"

Thank you for taking the time to read this testimony and for allowing this message to challenge your heart to step into God's purpose for your life. As God works through you and shows you amazing things, be sure to pass it forward and

---

share your own story of God's faithfulness so that you might inspire others to do the same.

Let us together make a difference in the lives of others around us. The mission field is not only on the other side of the world, it is also right where you are. Jesus told us to go into all the world and preach the Gospel. Ask yourself, is your neighborhood part of that world? And while you're at it, ask yourself who is supposed to be a light to those people today?

God bless you!

73701353R00090

Made in the USA
Columbia, SC
06 September 2019